Communications
in Computer and Information Sci

Jong Hyuk Park   Justin Zhan
Changhoon Lee   Guilin Wang
Tai-hoon Kim   Sang-Soo Yeo (Eds.)

Advances in Information Security and Its Application

Third International Conference, ISA 2009
Seoul, Korea, June 25-27, 2009
Proceedings

 Springer

Volume Editors

Jong Hyuk Park
Kyungnam University, Department of Computer Science and Engineering
Masan, Kyungnam, Korea
E-mail: parkjonghyuk1@hotmail.com

Justin Zhan
Carnegie Mellon CyLab Japan
Kobe, Japan
E-mail: justinzh@andrew.cmu.edu

Changhoon Lee
Hanshin University, School of Computer Engineering
Osan, Kyeong-Gi, Korea
E-mail: cryptography1@gmail.com

Guilin Wang
University of Birmingham, School of Computer Science
Birmingham, UK
E-mail: g.wang@cs.bham.ac.uk

Tai-hoon Kim
Hannam University, School of Multimedia
Daejeon, Korea
E-mail: taihoonn@empal.com

Sang-Soo Yeo
Mokwon University, Division of Computer Engineering
Daejeon, Korea
E-mail: ssyeo@msn.com

Library of Congress Control Number: Applied for

CR Subject Classification (1998): C.2, D.4.6, K.6.5, H.2.7, K.4.4

ISSN   1865-0929
ISBN-10   3-642-02632-X Springer Berlin Heidelberg New York
ISBN-13   978-3-642-02632-4 Springer Berlin Heidelberg New York

springer.com

© Springer-Verlag Berlin Heidelberg 2009
Printed in Germany

Typesetting: Camera-ready by author, data conversion by Scientific Publishing Services, Chennai, India
Printed on acid-free paper   SPIN: 12702763   06/3180   5 4 3 2 1 0

Preface

Welcome to the Third International Conference on Information Security and Assurance (ISA 2009). ISA 2009 was the most comprehensive conference focused on the various aspects of advances in information security and assurance. The concept of security and assurance is emerging rapidly as an exciting new paradigm to provide reliable and safe life services. Our conference provides a chance for academic and industry professionals to discuss recent progress in the area of communication and networking including modeling, simulation and novel applications associated with the utilization and acceptance of computing devices and systems. ISA 2009 was a successor of the First International Workshop on Information Assurance in Networks (IAN 2007, Jeju-island, Korea, December, 2007), and the Second International Conference on Information Security and Assurance (ISA 2008, Busan, Korea, April 2008). The goal of this conference is to bring together researchers from academia and industry as well as practitioners to share ideas, problems and solutions relating to the multifaceted aspects of information technology.

ISA 2009 contained research papers submitted by researchers from all over the world. In order to guarantee high-quality proceedings, we put extensive effort into reviewing the papers. All submissions were peer reviewed by at least three Program Committee members as well as external reviewers. As the quality of the submissions was quite high, it was extremely difficult to select the papers for oral presentation and publication in the proceedings of the conference. After extensive discussion and review, we finally decided to accept 16 regular papers for publication in CCIS volume 36 from 137 submitted papers. In addition, the full papers have been included in LNCS volume 5576. We believe that the chosen papers and topics provide novel ideas on future research activities.

It would have been impossible to organize our program without the help of many enthusiastic individuals. We owe special thanks to Sajid Hussain and Alan Chin-Chen Chang for serving as Workshop Co-chairs. We also thank all the members of the Program Committee (PC) who reviewed all of the papers submitted to the conference and provided their feedback to the authors. We appreciate the help of Hangbae Chang, Soo Kyun Kim, and Deok Gyu Lee for serving as the Local Chairs of the conference. They coordinated the use of the conference facilities and set up the registration website. And we would like to take this opportunity to thank all the authors and participants for their contributions to the conference.

Finally, we acknowledge the work of Doo-soon Park as Honorary Chair and the members of our International Advisory Board who have provided long-term guidance for the conference.

Jong Hyuk Park
Hsiao-Hwa Chen
M. Atiquzzaman
Changhoon Lee
Justin Zhan
Guilin Wang
Sang-Soo Yeo

Organization

Organizing Committee

Honorary Chair Doo-soon Park (SoonChunHyang University, Korea)

General Chairs Jong Hyuk Park (Kyungnam University, Korea)
Hsiao-Hwa Chen (National Sun Yat-Sen University, Taiwan)
M. Atiquzzaman (University of Oklahoma, USA)

International Advisory Board Peng Ning (North Carolina State University, USA)
Tai-hoon Kim (Hannam University, Korea)
Kyo Il Chung (ETRI, Korea)
Laurence T. Yang (St. Francis Xavier University, Canada)
Stefanos Gritzalis (University of the Aegean, Greece)
Alan Chin-Chen Chang (National Chung Cheng University, Taiwan)
Sung-Eon Cho (Sunchon National University, Korea)
Wai Chi Fang (National Chiao Tung University, Taiwan)
Tughrul Arslan (University of Edinburgh, UK)
Javier Lopez (University of Malaga, Spain)
Hamid R. Arabnia (The University of Georgia, USA)
Dominik Slezak (Infobright Inc., Canada)

Program Chairs Justin Zhan (CMU, USA)
Changhoon Lee (Hanshin University, Korea)
Guilin Wang (University of Birmingham, UK)

Publication Chair Sang-Soo Yeo (Mokwon University, Korea)

Program Committee

Alessandro Piva	Dharma P. Agrawal	Guojun Wang
Binod Vaidya	Dieter Gollmann	Hee-Jung Lee
Bo Zhu	Dorothy Denning	Ioannis G. Askoxylakis
Boniface Hicks	Duncan S. Wong	Isaac Agudo
Byoungcheon Lee	Edward Jung	Jaechul Sung
Chin-Chen Chang	Francesca Saglietti	Jan deMeer
Chunming Rong	Gail-Joon Ahn	Jeng-Shyang Pan
Claudio Ardagna	George Ghinea	Jianying Zhou
Dawu Gu	Golden G. Richard III	Jie Li

Table of Contents

Information Assurance and Its Application

Security Protocol and Its Application

Other Security Research

Designing Low-Cost Cryptographic Hardware for Wired- or Wireless Point-to-Point Connections

Sebastian Wallner

Hamburg University of Technology
Computer Technology Institute
D-21073 Hamburg, Germany
wallner@tu-harburg.de

Abstract. Science and industry consider non classical cryptographic technologies to provide alternative security solutions. They are motivated by strong restrictions as they are often present in embedded security scenarios and in application such as battery powered embedded systems and RFID devices with often severe resource limitations. We investigate the implementation of a low hardware complexity cryptosystem for lightweight (authenticated) symmetric key exchange, based on two new Tree Parity Machine Rekeying Architectures (TPMRAs). This work significantly extends and optimizes (number of gates) previously published results on TPMRAs. We evaluate characteristics of standard-cell ASIC design realizations as IP-core in 0.18-CMOS technology and an implementation into a standard bus controller with security features.

Keywords: Nonclassical cryptographic technologies, embedded security, bus encryption, streamcipher, authenticated symmetric key exchange.

1 Introduction

Alternative security primitives and new nonclassical cryptographic technologies and their investigation are recently stimulated by the strong restrictions present in resource limited devices and systems. Typically, battery powered devices, sensor networks, RFID or Near Field Communication (NFC) systems can impose severe size limitations and power consumption constraints. The available size e.g. for additional cryptographic hardware components in order to encrypt their communication channels (wired or wireless) is very limited [1], [2].

Strong cost limitations and performance requirements often result in a complete lack of security mechanisms. Therefore a challenge is to optimize a cost-performance ratio regarding the resource size (number of gates) and the communication channel bandwidth with respect to a given platform [3], [4], [5].

On the one hand additional gates for the implementation of cryptographic mechanisms also increases the cost. On the other hand, only security solutions with an appropriate security level tailored to the intended application field seem practicable. In practice, a necessary tradeoff between the level of security and the available resources has to be faced.

J.H. Park et al. (Eds.): ISA 2009, CCIS 36, pp. 1–10, 2009.

We suggest to discuss a hardware solution for lightweight authenticated symmetric key exchange based on the synchronization of Tree Parity Machines (TPMs) [6], [7]. Variable key lengths allow for flexible security levels especially in environments with moderate security concerns. For encryption, a streamcipher can be derived from the same concept with minimal additional effort [8]. We focus on a low hardware complexity IP-Core solution for secure data exchange over a standard bus or wireless communications channel between resource limited devices.

Recently the usage of the Tree Parity Machines and its underlying principle for a key exchange protocol was also used in applications such as OTP (One Time Password) authentication and secure authentication in WiMAX [9, 10].

2   Key Exchange and Stream Cipher by Tree Parity Machines

Symmetric key exchange via the synchronization of two interacting identically structured Tree Parity Machines is proposed by Kinzel and Kanter [11, 12].

The exchange protocol is realized by an interactive adaptation process between two interacting parties A and B. The TPM (see Figure 1a) consists of K independent summation units ($1 \leq k \leq K$) with non-overlapping inputs in a tree structure and a single parity unit at the output.

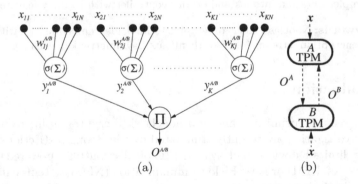

Fig. 1. (a) The Tree Parity Machine. A single output is calculated from the parity of the outputs of the summation units. (b) Outputs on commonly given inputs are exchanged between parties A and B for adaptation of their preliminary key.

Each summation unit receives different N inputs ($1 \leq j \leq N$), leading to an input field of size $K \cdot N$. The vector components are random variables with zero mean and unit variance. The output $O^{A/B}(t) \in \{-1,1\}$ (A/B denotes equivalent operations for A and B), given bounded coefficients (weights) $w_{kj}^{A/B}(t) \in [-L, L] \subseteq \mathbb{Z}$ (from input unit j to summation unit k) and common random inputs $x_{kj}(t) \in \{-1,1\}$, is calculated by a parity function of the signs of summations:

$$O^{A/B}(t) = \prod_{k=1}^{K} y_k^{A/B}(t) = \prod_{k=1}^{K} \sigma\left(\sum_{j=1}^{N} w_{kj}^{A/B}(t)\, x_{kj}(t)\right). \tag{1}$$

$\sigma(\cdot)$ denotes the sign-function.

Parties A and B start with an individual randomly generated secret initial vector $w_{kj}^{A/B}(t_0)$. These initially uncorrelated random variables become identical over time through the influence of the common inputs and the interactive adaptation as follows. After a set of $b > 1$ presented inputs, where b denotes the size of the bit package, the corresponding b TPM outputs (bits) $O^{A/B}(t)$ are exchanged over a public channel (see Figure 1b). When both parties adapted to produce each others outputs, they remain synchronous without further communication and continue to produce the same outputs on every commonly given input. This fact can be easily used to create a streamcipher [3, 8].

Given the parameters in [11] the average synchronization time is distributed. A so-called bit package variant (output bits are packed into a package) reduces transmissions of outputs by an order of magnitude down to a few packages (400 outputs result in thirteen 32-bit packages) [3, 6]. Synchrony is achieved only for common inputs. Keeping the common inputs secret between A and B can be used to have an entity authentication and authenticated key exchange which averts a Man-In-The-Middle attack (MITM) [3].

2.1 Security and Attacks

For the key exchange protocol without authentication, eavesdropping attacks have concurrently been proposed by [11] and Kanter, Kinzel et al. [14, 15].

These attacks can all be made arbitrarily costly and thus can be defeated by simply increasing the parameter L. The security increases proportional to L^2 while the probability of a successful attack decreases exponentially with L [14]. The approach is thus regarded computationally secure with respect to these attacks for sufficiently large L [14, 15].

The latest and best attack called "flipping-attack" does not seem to be affected by an increase of L but still by an increase of K [15].

Figure 2 provides the achievable security level in terms of the success probability of the flipping-attack, when scaling the parameter K [13]. Note that $2.9*10^{-39}$ is equivalent to guess a 128 bit key.

It is important to note, that all of the existing attacks refer to a non-authenticated key exchange, in which a MITM-attack on the symmetric key exchange principle is possible as well.

As previously indicated, synchrony is achieved only for common inputs x. Keeping the common inputs secret between A and B can be used to have an entity authentication and authenticated key exchange [3].

Additionally, the MITM-attack and all other currently known attacks [13, 14, 15] using TPMs are provably averted by this authentication.

Especially the MITM-attacker would have to be able to synchronize with respect to two sides (both parties), which is not possible if he does not even

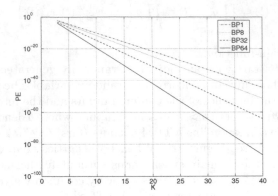

Fig. 2. Probability of a successful flipping attack PE vs. parameter K for different bit package sizes (BP)

produce the same inputs. An attack by learning cannot be successful if the inputs are different.

Important to note is that such a second secret does not represent any disadvantage to the symmetric approach, because some basic common information is always necessary for a secure symmetric key exchange. This fact is also important for the well known Diffie-Hellmann key exchange protocol.

3   Tree-Parity Machine Architecture Variants

With regard to a hardware implementation, the TPM uses only signs and bounded integers. The result of the outer product in (Equation 1) can be realized without multiplication. The product within the sum is only changing the sign of the coefficient. The most complex arithmetic structure to be implemented is thus an adder.

The Tree Parity Machine Rekeying Architectures are functionally separated into two main structures. One structure comprises the Handshake/Key Controller, the Bitpackage Unit and the Watchdog, the other structure contains the Tree Parity Machine Unit for calculating the basic TPM functions. Figure 3 gives an overview of the hardware structure.

The Handshake/Key Controller Unit handles the key transmission with an additional encryption unit and the bit package exchange process with the other party by using a simple request and acknowledge handshake protocol. In both architectures, the Bitpackage Unit partitions the output bits (Equation 1) from the TPM unit in tighter bit slices. The Bitpackage Unit handles arbitrary bit package lengths (depending on the key length) for different parallel data exchange buses. The Watchdog supervises the synchronization between the two parties, which is determined by the chosen parameters and the random initial values of the parties. The Iteration Counter in the Watchdog counts the number of exchanged output bits. It generates a synchronization error (Sync Error),

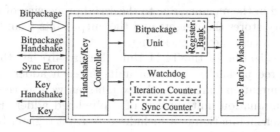

Fig. 3. Basic diagram of the Handshake/Key Controller with the Watchdog and the Bitpackage Unit. As shown later, the TPM unit may include a parallel or serial TPM computation structure.

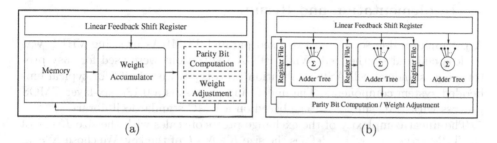

Fig. 4. Overview of the Tree Parity Machine Rekeying Architectures. (a) shows the serial TPMRA, (b) shows the parallel TPMRA.

if there is no synchronization within a specific number of iterations. The Sync Counter is needed to determine the synchronization of the TPMs by comparing and counting equal output bit packages. It is increased when a sent bit package and the corresponding received bit package is identical and otherwise cleared. A synchronization is recognized when a specified number of equal bit packages is reached.

The serially realized TPM structure to calculate a parity bit is a fully parameterizable hardware structure. The parameters K, N and L as well as the bit package length can be set arbitrarily in order to adopt this architecture variant for different system environments.

The serial TPM Unit consists of a TPM control state machine, a Linear Feedback Shift Register (LFSR), a Weight Accumulator, a Parity Bit Computation and Weight Adjustment Unit and a memory (Figure 4a). The TPM controller is realized as simple finite state machine (omitted for clarity in Figure 4a).

It handles the initialization of the TPM, the adaptation with the parity bits of the bit package from the other party and controls the parity calculation and weight adjustment. The LFSR generates the pseudo random bits for the inputs $x_{kj}(t)$ of the TPM. The Parity Bit Computation computes the output parity and the Weight Adjustment Unit accomplishes the adaptation. The Weight Accumulator computes each sum of the summation units. Each partial result must be temporarily stored in the memory, due to the serial processing of the summation units. The memory stores the weights and the output bits from the summation units in order to process the bit packaging.

The parallel realization of the TPM Unit (Figure 4b) has the same overall structure, but three parallel summation units in each adder tree. A register bank for each summation unit holds the weights as well as the parity bits of each unit. The summation unit consists of a pipelined adder tree designed to add N inputs. Each summation unit includes a $N \cdot L$-bit register bank due to the need for parallel availability of data.

In contrast to the serial TPM realization, the computation of the parity and weight adjustment of each summation unit is also performed in parallel.

4   Implementation and Results

A parameterizable serial and two fixed parallel TPMRAs by using VHDL was re-designed and synthesized. While FPGA realizations were used for easy prototyping, standard cell ASIC realization prototypes were build for typical embedded system components. The underlying process is a 0.18μ six-layer CMOS process with $1.8V$ supply voltage based on a UMC standardcell library.

The linear complexity of the exchange protocol scales with the size $K \cdot N$ of the TPM structure, which defines the size $K \cdot N \cdot L$ of the key. We chose $K = 3$, a maximal $N = 88$ and $L = 3$ for the serial architecture. This leads to a key size of up to 1056 bit.

The parallel TPM realization (with $K = 3$ and $N = 11$ fixed) has a key length of 132 bit with $L = 3$. The number of gates (Figure 5a) of the serial TPMRA scales approximately linear due to the linear increase in required memory. Note, that most of the area is consumed by the memory, because of the necessary storage of partial results. Yet, this influence is minor for an ASIC realization, because here registers can be mapped more efficiently than on current FPGA architectures.

The achievable clock-frequency (Figure 5b) ranges between 159 and 312 MHz for the investigated key lengths with internal memory. Additionally, we established the throughput (i.e. keys per second) subject to the average synchronization time of 400 iterations for different key lengths in Figure 5c. A practically finite channel capacity is neglected here.

The serial TPMRA achieves a maximal theoretical throughput in the kHz-range. After the initial synchronization the streamcipher mode, also shown in Figure 5c, allows to increase the throughput by two orders of magnitude due to the reduced number of cycles used in the TPM streamcipher mode [3, 6, 7].

In order to compare the proposed solution with different streamciphers, we synthesized two parallel TPMRAs. For this purpose, a TPMRA variant with calculates 16 bit/cycle and a architecture variant with 32 bit/cycle was synthesized. Figure 6 shows the number of gates and throughput results of the parallel TPMRA in comparison to different streamciphers in bit/cycle. For a better comparison, the design constraints are set in order to reach a maximum

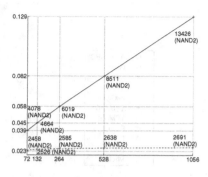 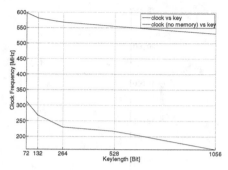

(a) Area $[mm^2]$ vs. key length $[bit]$ with (b) Speed $[MHz]$ vs. key length $[bit]$ with and and without internal memory (dashed) without internal memory (dashed)

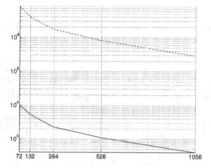

(c) Average key exchange rate and stream cipher bit-rate rate $[Hz]$ (log-scaled) vs. key length $[bit]$(idealized infinite channel bandwidth)

Fig. 5. Serial TPMRA area-optimized design results

clock frequency of 100 MHz. The design results of the well known streamciphers E0, A5/1 and RC4 where chosen from [16], other results were taken from the eSTREAM-Project [17]. Furthermore gate counts from a 100 MHz AES variant in an equivalent CMOS technology is illustrated. The AES runs in CBC mode as a streamcipher [18]. The TPMRAs with 16 bit/cycle and 32 bit/cycle are marked with TPMS16 and TPMS32.

The AES streamcipher mode achieves 11.5 bit/clock. The design has approximately 17.000 gates compared to the TPMS16 variant (16 bit/cycle, 17.500 gates). The TPMS32 variant (32 bit/cycle, 22717 gates) reaches the same throughput as Phelix and ZkCrypt. The number of gates are slightly higher when compared to Phelix.

Grain has a throughput of 16 bit/cycle and ZkCrypt a throughput of 32 bit/cycle both with nearly the same number of gates. In comparison to the TPMS16, Grain has a lower gate count. As shown the gates/throughput ratio

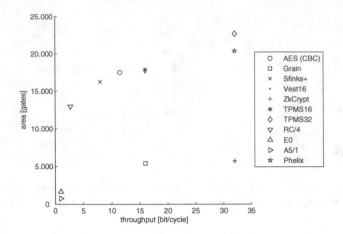

Fig. 6. Number of gates for the parallel TPMRA and different streamciphers vs throughput (bit/cycle)

from Grain and ZkCrypt is better in comparison to RC4 and AES. In comparison to the alternative streamciphers, the two parallel TPMRAs achieves a higher throughput with only a small gate increase.

In addition to the TPMRA streamcipher mode, it provides an authenticated key exchange. No other streamciphers offer this feature.

5   TPMRA Bus Controller Implementation

An illustration how to implement the TPMRA into a bus controller in order to ensure bus communication between different hardware components will be discussed in the following.

Figure 7a shows a structure proposal of a typical bus system with several bus participants. In order to ensure bus communication each bus participant needs to implement a TPMRA core (see Figure 7a, shared trusted area). Additionally, the core allows key exchange and the authentication of bus participants.

It can be used to encrypt the bus communication on the physical/wireless bus by using the TPM streamcipher mode. The proposed solution is fully transparent and runs independent from other processes in the background. Typically, the bus protocol could be untouched.

Figure 7b gives a deeper insight of a bus controller with security features. For encryption the streamcipher mode based on the TPM principle is used. In order to enhance the quality of the streamcipher data stream, an additional hash function improves the quality of the streamcipher key stream [8]. A dedicated controller handles whether confidential data to other bus participants are encrypted or plane. If security is needed both key- and data streams are xord in order to have encrypted data streams (see Figure 7b).

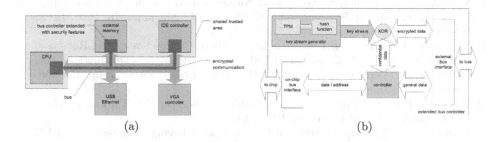

(a)   (b)

Fig. 7. (a) Implementation of a secure bus controller into a bus system with different bus participants. The TPMRA core is illustrated as a black box in each bus participants. (b) The internal structure of a secure bus controller including the TPM core for key exchange and streamcipher is shown on the left upper side. Additionally a hash function is implemented in order to improve the quality of the key stream. An internal controller decides whether encrypted or general data are transmitted to the external bus by snooping dedicated memory addresses.

Typically the bus encryption mode can be activated if dedicated addresses are selected. This simple principle allows to encrypt arbitrary addresses or entire address ranges in a processor memory map.

6   Conclusions

A nonclassical cryptographic technology for low hardware complexity lightweight authenticated symmetric key exchange, based on two variants of Tree Parity Machine Rekeying Architectures (TPMRAs) was suggested. A serial TPMRA variant (132 bit key) needs only 1064 NAND2 gates. Additionally a proposal to implement the TPMRA into a bus controller was described.

We regard the TPMRAs as IP-cores for lightweight authenticated key exchange including a streamcipher generator both for wired or wireless communication channels in embedded system environments. A particular focus can be typical chip to chip bus systems (AMBA Bus) or wireless transponder-based applications such as RFID-systems as well as devices in ad-hoc or sensor networks, in which a small area for cryptographic components is mandatory. Side channel attacks (SPA, DPA) and power consumption for different key lengths must be investigated in future.

References

[1] Stanford, V.: Pervasive computing goes the last hundred feet with RFID systems. Pervasive Computing, IEEE Computer Science, 9–14 (2003)
[2] Stajano, F.: Security in pervasive computing. In: Hutter, D., Müller, G., Stephan, W., Ullmann, M. (eds.) Security in Pervasive Computing. LNCS, vol. 2802, pp. 6–8. Springer, Heidelberg (2004)

[3] Muehlbach, S., Wallner, S.: Secure and Authenticated Communication in Chip-Level Microcomputer Bus Systems with Tree Parity Machines. In: Proc. IEEE IC-SAMOS, Greece, pp. 201–208 (July 2007)

[4] Bogdanov, A.A., Knudsen, L.R., Leander, G., Paar, C., Poschmann, A., Robshaw, M.J.B., Seurin, Y., Vikkelsoe, C.: PRESENT: An ultra-lightweight block cipher. In: Paillier, P., Verbauwhede, I. (eds.) CHES 2007. LNCS, vol. 4727, pp. 450–466. Springer, Heidelberg (2007)

[5] Paar, C.: Past and future of cryptographic engineering. In: Tutorial at HOT CHIPS 2003, Stanford University, USA (2003)

[6] Volkmer, M., Wallner, S.: Tree Parity Machine Rekeying Architectures. IEEE Transactions on Computers 54(4), 421–427 (2005)

[7] Volkmer, M., Wallner, S.: A Key Establishment IP-Core for Ubiquitous Computing. In: Proc. 1st Int. Workshop on Secure and Ubiquitous Networks, SUN 2005, Denmark 2005, pp. 241–245. IEEE Computer Society, Los Alamitos (2005)

[8] Volkmer, M., Wallner, S.: Lightweight Key Exchange and Stream Cipher based solely on Tree Parity Machines. In: ECRYPT Workshop on RFID and Lightweight Crypto, Graz University of Technology, Austria, pp. 102–113 (July 2005)

[9] Chen, T., Huang, S.H.: Tree Parity Machine-based One-time Password Authentication Schemes. In: Int. Joint Conference on Neural Networks, Hong Kong, June 1-6 (2008)

[10] Dong, H., Yu Yan, W.: Secure Authentication on WiMAX with Neural Cryptography. In: Int. Conference on Information Security and Assurance (ISA) 2008, pp. 366–369, April 24-26 (2008)

[11] Kanter, I., Kinzel, W., Kanter, E.: Secure exchange of information by synchronization of neural networks. Europhysics Letters 57(1), 141–147 (2002)

[12] Ruttor, A., Kinzel, W., Kanter, I.: Dynamics of neural cryptography. Phys. Rev. E 75 (2007)

[13] Klimov, A.B., Mityagin, A., Shamir, A.: Analysis of neural cryptography. In: Zheng, Y. (ed.) ASIACRYPT 2002. LNCS, vol. 2501, pp. 288–298. Springer, Heidelberg (2002)

[14] Mislovaty, R., Perchenok, Y., Kanter, I., Kinzel, W.: Secure key exchange protocol with an absence of injective functions. Phys. Rev. E 66 (2002)

[15] Kanter, I., et al.: Cooperating attackers in neural cryptography. Phys Rev. E 69 (2004)

[16] Batina, L., Lano, J., Mentens, N., Ors, S.B., Preneel, B., Verbauwhede, I.: Energy, performance, area versus security tradeoffs for streamciphers. Catholic University Leuven (2005)

[17] eSTREAM: ECRYPT, http://www.ecrypt.eu.org/stream

[18] AES Core: CAST-INC, http://www.cast-inc.com

A Security Metrics Development Method for Software Intensive Systems

Reijo M. Savola

VTT Technical Research Centre of Finland, Kaitoväylä 1, 90570 Oulu, Finland
Reijo.Savola@vtt.fi

Abstract. It is a widely accepted management principle that an activity cannot be managed well if it cannot be measured. Carefully designed security metrics can be used to offer evidence of the security behavior of the system under development or operation. We propose a systematic and holistic method for security metrics development for software intensive systems. The approach is security requirement-centric and threat and vulnerability-driven. The high-level security requirements are expressed in terms of lower-level measurable components applying a decomposition approach. Next, feasibility of the basic measurable components is investigated, and more detailed metrics developed based on selected components.

Keywords: security metrics, security requirements, security level.

1 Introduction

The increasing complexity of software-intensive and telecommunication products, together with pressure from security and privacy legislation, are increasing the need for adequately validated security solutions. In order to obtain evidence of the information security performance of systems needed for the validation, services or products, systematic approaches to measuring security are needed. The field of defining security metrics systematically is very young. Because the current practice of security is still a highly diverse field, holistic and widely accepted measurement and metrics approaches are still missing.

The main contribution of this study is introduce a novel method for security metrics development based on threats, security requirements, use case information and decomposition of security goals.

The rest of this paper is organized in the following way. Section 2 gives a short introduction to security metrics. Section 3 introduces the proposed security metrics development process. Section 4 discusses threat and vulnerability analysis, and the next section security requirements. Section 6 describes decomposition of security requirements. Section 7 explains issues important in the measurement architecture and evidence collection. Section 8 presents related work and finally, Section 9 summarizes the study with some future research questions and conclusions.

J.H. Park et al. (Eds.): ISA 2009, CCIS 36, pp. 11–16, 2009.
© Springer-Verlag Berlin Heidelberg 2009

2 Security Metrics

Security metrics and measurements can be used for decision support, especially in assessment and prediction. When using metrics for prediction, mathematical models and algorithms are applied to the collection of measured data (e.g. regression analysis) to predict the security performance. The target of security measurement can be, e.g., an organization, its processes and resources, or a product or its subsystem. In general, there are two main categories of security metrics: (i) security metrics based on threats but not emphasizing attacker behavior, and (ii) security metrics predicting and emphasizing attacker behavior. In this study, we concentrate in the former type of metrics. Security metrics properties can be quantitative or qualitative, objective or subjective, static or dynamic, absolute or relative, or direct or indirect. According to ISO 9126 standard [1], a direct measure is a measure of an attribute that does not depend upon a measure of any other attribute. On the other hand, an indirect measure is derived from measures of one or more other attributes. See [2] and [3] for examples of security metrics.

The feasibility of measuring security and developing security metrics to present actual security phenomena has been criticized in many contributions. In designing a security metric, one has to be conscious of the fact that the metric simplifies a complex socio-technical situation down to numbers or partial orders. McHugh [4] is skeptical of the side effects of such simplification and the lack of scientific proof. Bellovin [5] remarks that defining metrics is hard, if not infeasible, because an attacker's effort is often linear, even in cases where exponential security work is needed. Another source of challenges is that luck plays a major role [6] especially in the weakest links of information security solutions. Those pursuing the development of a security metrics program should think of themselves as pioneers and be prepared to adjust strategies as experience dictates [7].

3 Proposed Security Metrics Development Process

In this study, we use the following iterative process for security metrics development, partly based on [8]. The steps for the process are as follows:

1. Carry out threat and vulnerability analysis. Identify and elaborate threats of the system under investigation and its use environment. If enough information is available, identify known or suspected vulnerabilities. This work can continue iteratively as more details of the target will be known.
2. Define and prioritize security requirements, including related requirements critical from security point of view, in a holistic way based on the threat and vulnerability analysis. The most critical security requirements should be paid the most attention. Pay attention to the simplicity and unambiguity of the requirements.
3. Identify *Basic Measurable Components* (BMC) from the higher-level security requirements using a decomposition approach. BMCs relate the metrics to be developed to security requirements.
4. Develop measurement architecture for on-line metrics and evidence collection mechanisms for off-line metrics.

5. Select BMCs to be used as the basis for detailed metrics based on their feasibility and criticality.
6. Define and validate detailed security metrics, and the functionalities and processes where they are used.

All steps are iterative and the sequence of the steps can be varied depending on the availability of information required. Steps 1 and 2 should be started as early as possible in the development process and elaborated iteratively as the system design gets more mature. Steps 3 and 4 can be carried out in parallel to each other. Step 4 can be initiated already during the architectural design phase of the system or service.

4 Threat and Vulnerability Analysis

Threat analysis is the process of determining the relevant threats to an SUI (System under Investigation). The outcome of the threat analysis process is preferably a prioritized description of the threat situations. In practice, there are many ways to carry out threat analysis, from simply enumerating threats to modeling them in a more rigorous way. The extent of threat analysis depends, e.g., on the criticality of the use cases in the SUI. The following threat and vulnerability analysis process can be used, based on the Microsoft threat risk modeling process [9]: (i) identify security objectives, (ii) survey the SUI architecture, (iii) decompose the SUI architecture to identify functions and entities with impact to security, (iv) identify threats, and (v) identify vulnerabilities.

The security objectives can be decomposed, e.g., to identity, financial, reputation, privacy and regulatory and availability categories [10]. There are many different sources of risk guidance that can be used in developing the security objectives, such as laws, regulations, standards, legal agreements and information security policies.

Threats are the goals of the adversary and for a threat to exist it must have a target asset. To identify threats, the following questions can be asked [11]:

1. How can the adversary use or manipulate the asset to modify or control the system, retrieve or manipulate information within the system, cause the system to fail or become unusable or to gain additional rights?
2. Can the adversary access the asset without being audited and skip any access control checks, and appear to be another user?

The threats can be classified using a suitable model like STRIDE (Spoofing, Tampering, Repudiation, Information Disclosure, Denial of Service, Elevation of Privilege) [9]. DREAD (Damage Potential, Reproducibility, Exploitability, Affected Users, Discoverability) [9] is a classification scheme for quantifying, comparing and prioritizing the amount of risk presented by each evaluated threat. Vulnerability analysis can be carried out after appropriate technological choices have been made. In vulnerability analysis, well-known vulnerability listings and repositories such as CWE (Common Weakness Enumeration) [12] and OWASP (Open Web Application Security Project) Top 10 [10] can be used. Metrics from Common Vulnerability Scoring System (CVSS) [13] can be used to depict how easy or hard it is to access and exploit a known vulnerability in the system.

5 Security Requirements

Security requirements derive from *threats*, *policies* and *environment properties*. If they are derived from threats, they are actually countermeasures. Security policies are security relevant directives, objectives and design choices that are seen necessary for the system under investigation. Environment properties contribute to the security of the SUI from outside – either advancing or reducing it. The explanation for the security-advancing effect of the environment is that it could to contain a countermeasure solution against a threat, outside the SUI. In general, every security risk due to a threat chosen to be cancelled or mitigated must have a countermeasure in the collection of security requirements.

A security requirement of the SUI r_i is derived from applicable threat(s) θ_i, policy or policies p_i and the environment properties e_i:

$$r_i = (\theta_i, p_i, e_i), \quad r_i \in R, \theta_i \in \Theta, p_i \in P, e_i \in E, \tag{1}$$

where R is the collection of all security requirements of SUI, Θ is the collection of all security threats chosen to be cancelled or mitigated, P is the collection of all security policies applied to SUI, and E is the collection of all environment properties that contribute to the security of the SUI from outside.

In general, the state of practice in defining security requirements is not at matured level. According to Firesmith [14], the most current software requirement specifications are either (i) totally silent regarding security, (ii) merely specify vague security goals, or (iii) specify commonly used security mechanisms (e.g., encryption and firewalls) as architectural constraints. In the first case security is not taken into account in an adequately early phase of design. In the second case vague security goals (like "the application shall be secure") are not testable requirements. The third case may unnecessarily tie architectural decisions too early, resulting in an inappropriate security mechanism.

Security requirements are often conceived solely as non-functional requirements along with such aspects as performance and reliability within the requirements engineering community [15]. From the security engineering viewpoint this is a too simplified way of thinking; security cannot be represented only by non-functional requirements since security goals often motivate new functionality, such as monitoring, intrusion detection and access control, which, in turn, need functional requirements. Unfortunately, satisfactory approaches to capturing and analyzing non-functional requirements have yet to mature [16].

6 Decomposing Requirements

The core activity in the proposed security metrics development process is in decomposing the security requirements. In the following, we discuss the decomposition process and give an example of it.

The following decomposition process (based on [17]) is used to identify measurable components from the security requirements:

1. Identify successive components from each security requirement (goal) that *contribute to the success* of the goal.
2. Examine the subordinate nodes to see if further decomposition is needed. If so, repeat the process with the subordinate nodes as current goals, breaking them down to their essential components.
3. Terminate the decomposition process when none of the leaf nodes can be decomposed any further, or further analysis of these components is no longer necessary.

When the decomposition terminates, all leaf nodes should be measurable components. In the following, we decompose the requirements presented above and discuss the results. Since adaptive security contains higher-level requirements, we leave it to the last. It is easier to investigate the six lower-level requirement categories first. Fig. 1 shows an example of authentication decomposition.

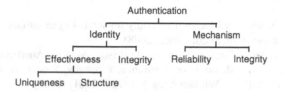

Fig. 1. Example decomposition of authentication

Different authentication mechanisms (e.g. password authentication and various forms of biometrics and any combination) can be used for different authentication needs. Fig. 1 commends that the security level of authentication mechanisms is depending on their level of reliability and integrity. There are many ways to use metrics and their combinations. Different component measures of the same security objective – here authentication performance A – can be summed up using weighted summation [8]:

$$A = w_0 \cdot u + w_1 \cdot s + w_2 \cdot id + w_3 \cdot r + w_4 \cdot ia, \tag{2}$$

where w_j, $j = 0,1,..4$, is the weight of the component, u = uniqueness of the identity, s = structure of identity, id = integrity of identity, r = reliability of authentication mechanism and ia = integrity of authentication mechanism.

7 Measurement Architecture and Evidence Collection

In the case of on-line metrics, the measurement architecture and data flow needs to be designed, in parallel to the overall architectural and data flow design of the SUI. Similarly, in the case of off-line metrics, the evidence collection mechanisms and criteria need to be planned. In many cases, on-line and off-line measurements can be dependent on each other.

8 Related Work

Wang and Wulf [17] describe a general-level framework for measuring system security based on a decomposition approach. CVSS [13] (Common Vulnerability Scoring

System) is a global initiative designed to provide an open and standardized method for rating information technology vulnerabilities from a practical point of view. NIST's Software Assurance Metrics and Tool Evaluation (SAMATE) project [18] seeks to help answer various questions on software assurance, tools and metrics. OWASP (Open Web Application Security Project) [10] contains an active discussion forum on security metrics. More security metrics approaches are surveyed in [2] and [3].

Acknowledgments. The work presented in this paper has been carried out in the GEMOM FP7 research project, partly funded by the European Commission.

References

1. ISO/IEC 9126-4: Software Engineering – Product Quality – Part 4: Quality in Use Metrics (2000)
2. Savola, R.: A Novel Security Metrics Taxonomy for R&D Organisations. In: ISSA 2008, July 7-9, 2008, Johannesburg, South Africa (2008)
3. Herrmann, D.S.: Complete Guide to Security and Privacy Metrics. Auerbach Publ. (2007)
4. McHugh, J.: Quantitative Measures of Assurance: Prophecy, Process or Pipedream? In: WISSSR, ACSA and MITRE, Williamsburg, VA (May 2001) (2002)
5. Bellovin, S.M.: On the Brittleness of Software and the Infeasibility of Security Metrics. IEEE Security & Privacy 2006, 96 (2006)
6. Burris, P., King, C.: A Few Good Security Metrics. METAGroup, Inc. (2000)
7. Payne, S.C.: A Guide to Security Metrics. SANS Institute (2006)
8. Savola, R., Abie, H.: Identification of Basic Measurable Security Components for a Distributed Messaging System. In: SECURWARE 2009, Athens, Greece, June 18-23, 2009, 8 p. (2009)
9. Howard, M., LeBlanc, D.: Writing Secure Code, 2nd edn. Microsoft Press (2003)
10. OWASP (Open Web Application Security Project): Threat Risk Modeling (2009), http://owasp.org
11. Swiderski, F., Snyder, W.: Threat Modeling. Microsoft Press (2004)
12. CWE (Common Weakness Enumeration) (2009), http://cwe.mitre.org
13. Schiffman, M.: A Complete Guide to the Common Vulnerability Scoring System (CVSS). White paper (2009)
14. Firesmith, D.: Specifying Reusable Security Requirements. Journal of Object Technology 3(1), 61–75 (2004)
15. Chung, L., Nixon, B.A., Yu, E.: Using Quality Requirements to Systematically Develop Quality Software. In: 4th Int. Conf. on Software Quality, McLean, VA (October 1994)
16. Nuseibeh, B., Easterbrook, S.: Requirements Engineering: A Roadmap, The Future of Software Engineering. In: Finkelstein, A. (ed.) ICSE 2000 (Special vol.), pp. 35–46 (2000)
17. Wang, C., Wulf, W.A.: Towards a Framework for Security Measurement. In: 20th National Information Systems Security Conference, Baltimore, MD, October 1997, pp. 522–533 (1997)
18. Plack, P.E.: SAMATE's Contribution to Information Assurance. IANewsletter 9(2) (2006)

The ISDF Framework: Integrating
Security Patterns and Best Practices

Abdulaziz Alkussayer and William H. Allen

Department of Computer Science
Florida Institute of Technology
Melbourne, FL, USA
alkussaa@fit.edu, wallen@fit.edu

Abstract. The rapid growth of communication and globalization has changed the software engineering process. Security has become a crucial component of any software system. However, software developers often lack the knowledge and skills needed to develop secure software. Clearly, the creation of secure software requires more than simply mandating the use of a secure software development lifecycle, the components produced by each stage of the lifecycle must be correctly implemented for the resulting system to achieve its intended goals. In this paper, we demonstrate that a more effective approach to the development of secure software can result from the integration of carefully selected security patterns into appropriate stages of the software development lifecycle to ensure that security designs are correctly implemented. The goal of this work is to provide developers with an Integrated Security Development Framework (ISDF) that can assist them in building more secure software intuitively.

1 Introduction

Until recently, security in software development was viewed as a patch deployed to solve security breaches, or sometimes as an enhancement to an already completed software package. As a result, security considerations were located towards the end of the development lifecycle; particularly as add-on mechanisms and techniques before the system was deployed at the client's premises. Security issues were often raised only after some undetected vulnerability had been compromised. It was not yet understood that developing secure software requires a careful injection of security consideration into each stage of the software development lifecycle [1,2,3,4]. However, once the importance of designed-in security was recognized, attention was directed towards improving the development process by considering security as a requirement instead of a corrective measure.

The inspiration for our previously proposed ISDF framework [5] came from recognizing the existence of two common software development pitfalls: i) security is often only an afterthought in software development; ii) many security breaches exploit well-known security problems. The first issue can only be corrected by mandating the use of a secure development lifecycle to incorporate

J.H. Park et al. (Eds.): ISA 2009, CCIS 36, pp. 17–28, 2009.
© Springer-Verlag Berlin Heidelberg 2009

security considerations across all software development stages. The second must be solved by ensuring that software developers make use of security patterns to avoid insecure development practices.

Fortunately, software security engineering has matured in recent years. Software developers have become more conscious of the fact that security has to be built within the system rather than on the system [4,6,7]. Thus, software security research has been active in two areas: improving engineering best-practices and increasing the use of security knowledge during development.

To address the first area, significant work has been done to formulate a methodology that considers security throughout the secure software development lifecycle (SDLC). The objective is to provide a set of development guidelines and rules on how to build more secure software. Among the many advantages of such methodologies is the ability to equip software developers with easy-to-follow security guidelines. These methodologies represent the best known engineering practices for building secure software. Two well-documented approaches are the Security Development Lifecycle (SDL) [8] and Software Security TouchPoints [9]. A recent discussion of both approaches can be found in the Fundamental Secure Software Development initiative by SAFECode[1] [10].

It has recently been recognized that security knowledge may be encapsulated within security patterns. A pattern describes a time-tested generic solution to a recurring problem within a specific context [11]. Since 1977 when patterns were first introduced by Alexander, et al. [12], they have become a very popular method of encapsulating knowledge in many disciplines. In software engineering, design patterns and security patterns have gained significant attention from the research community. Moreover, design patterns have become increasingly popular since publication of the Gang-of-Four (GoF) book [13]. Although design patterns have been widely adopted in most of today's development libraries and programming tools, the use of security patterns is more recent. They gained popularity following the seminal work by Yoder and Barcalow [14] which presented seven architectural patterns that are useful in developing the security aspects of a system. They used natural language and (GoF) templates to describe their patterns. Since then, many other security patterns have been published. Although many of the published security patterns are considered to be merely guidelines or principals [15], security patterns have been proven to be effective methods of dealing with security problems in a software system. Nevertheless, significant effort and security expertise are needed to properly apply them to a real software development situation.

In this paper, we demonstrate how the ISDF framework can be used to integrate the two independent security solutions mentioned above. First, we describe how the ISDF framework incorporates the best features of existing secure SDLCs. Then, we explain a four-stage utilization process for employing security patterns during the development lifecycle. Finally, we present a practical example that illustrates the benefits of using the ISDF framework during software development

---

[1] SAFECode is a global industry-led effort to identify and promote best-practices for developing and delivering more secure software and hardware services.

and shows that our combined approach consolidates the secure development best practices that are incorporated into a secure SDLC with the security knowledge built into security patterns. The authors are aware that the addition of a metrics component is necessary to measure the effectiveness of the framework and are working to incorporate security metrics into the ISDF. The results of our metrics-related work will be presented in a future paper.

The rest of this paper is structured as follows. Section 2 provides a brief overview of secure software development and security patterns. Section 3 provides an overview of related work. Section 4 describes the ISDF framework. Section 5 presents a practical example that illustrates the use of the ISDF framework to effectively develop more secure software. Section 6 contains our conclusions and a brief discussion of future work.

2   Background

In recent literature, a number of approaches for developing secure software are discussed. The Fundamental Secure Software Development guide by SAFECode [10] presents a six-phase software development cycle and discusses the best industry practices required during each phase to produce more secure software. The development phases are: requirements, design, programming, testing, code integrity and handling, and documentation [10]. This guide serves as the main source of security best practices that are incorporated into our framework.

Two well-known secure development methodologies are Microsoft's SDL, which first appeared as a result of the Trustworthy Computing Initiative in 2002 [8], and Software Security TouchPoints, which was proposed by Gary McGraw in 2004 [9]. Although there are differences between these methodologies, they agree on three key points [6,7,10]:

1. Advocate security education
2. Risk management is essential
3. Utilization of best practices is crucial

Microsoft's SDL is based on thirteen stages, spanning the entire development lifecycle [6]. These stages are: education & awareness, project inception, defining and following design best practices, product risk assessment, risk analysis, creating security documents/tools/best-practice for customer, secure coding policies, secure testing policies, the security push, the final security review, security response planning, product release, and security response execution. The software development artifacts mandated by Microsoft's SDL methodology are: requirements, design, implementation, verification, release, and support & services [6].

The Software Security Touchpoints methodology depends on the following seven best practices: code review, architectural risk analysis, penetration testing, risk-based security testing, abuse cases, security requirements, and security operations [9]. It also mandates six development phases: requirements and use cases, architecture and design, test plan, code, tests and test results, and feedback from the field [7].

Security patterns have become a reliable approach for effectively addressing security considerations during implementation of a software system. The security patterns book [11] includes forty six patterns. Twenty five of these security patterns address security issues during the design phase. Many of these patterns are well structured and hence the use of UML diagrams to represent such patterns is common. For example, Fernandez and Pan [16] used UML diagrams to illustrate four security patterns: Authorization, Role Based Access Control, Multilevel Security, and File Authorization patterns.

There are also several model-based security patterns. Hatebue et al. [17] presented security patterns using the Security Problem Frame which is used to capture and analyze security requirements. Horvath and Dorges [18] use Petri Nets to model patterns for multi-agent systems, such as the Sandbox and Message Secrecy patterns. Supaporn et al. [19] proposed a more formal method by constructing an extended-BNF-based grammar of security requirements from security patterns.

The use of security patterns during development is essential for building secure software. The richness of the number of security patterns published is encouraging. However, in many cases pattern designers do not provide clear information on when to apply their patterns within the software development lifecycle [20] and selection of the right pattern at the right development stage is not an easy task.

3   Related Work

Researchers have begun to focus on integrating security patterns into a software development lifecycle. For example, Aprville and Pourzandi [21] investigated the use of security patterns and UMLsec [22] in some phases of a secure software development lifecycle but were hampered by the limited range of patterns available at the time. They also did not describe how patterns could be incorporated into a secure SDL to create a development framework.

Valenzuela recommended a methodology that integrates the ISO 17799 (an international Information Security Standard) with a software development lifecycle [23]. This approach proposes parallel security activities for each stage of the SDL and included a mapping of each stage to the appropriate phase of the ISO 17799 process.

Fernandez et al. [24] proposed a methodology that incorporates security patterns in all development stages of their own lifecycle. Their approach includes guidelines for integrating security from the requirements phase through analysis, design, and implementation. In a more recent paper, Fernandez et al. [25] proposed a combination of three similar methodologies into a single unified approach to build secure systems using patterns, but did not integrate them into an industry-recognized Secure SDL.

Existing studies have focused on using either security patterns or best practices - or a loose combination of the two - to build secure software. However, none have explored the need for a concrete method to incorporate the full strength of the two approaches. In the following section, we present a framework that integrates the strengths of both of these well-proven software development techniques.

4 The ISDF Framework

The Integrated Security Development Framework (ISDF) consists of two main components, as shown in Figure 1. The first component is the secure software development best practice, represented on the left-hand side of Figure 1. The second component is a four-stage security pattern utilization process which appears in the right-hand side of the figure. The left hand side of Figure 1 shows the ISDF mandating a development lifecycle. However, this framework does not represent a particular development lifecycle and hence a conventional development model with six phases is used. These phases are very common in any development model. Also, the short activities included in each phase are summarized from [6,7,10] collectively. These activities represent the best engineering practices for developing secure software.

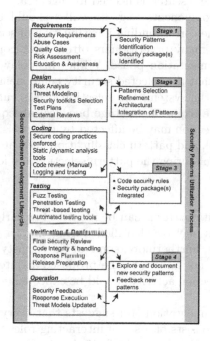

Fig. 1. Integrated Security Development Framework

The relation between the best practices activities and security patterns activity is bidirectional. Thus, the key success factor for seamless integration involves interweaving best practices and security pattern activities at every development stage.

Next, we explain how our framework effectively merges security patterns into the secure software development process.

4.1   Requirements Stage

In this stage, security patterns are selected based on the security requirements and on an analysis of potential threats that are determined from the preliminary risk assessment. For example, Access Control patterns and Identification and Authorization patterns [11] can be identified during this stage. Unfortunately, many practitioners unconsciously postpone the decision of identifying and selecting security patterns to the design phase. Since security patterns evolved from design patterns, however, identifying security patterns reveals more than just a design solution. It places security constraints on the system as a whole, as well as on its subcomponents. These security constraints must be rationalized by measurable security requirements and their associated risks must be mitigated. The relationship between security requirements and security patterns is vital. Some researchers [17,19] have investigated this relationship and proposed promising solutions. However, more research is needed in this area.

Moreover, security components (e.g. firewalls) should be identified at this stage in parallel with the corresponding identification of security tools based on best practices. In fact, many practitioners often don't consider security components until the implementation phase. While this delay is somewhat understandable in the sense that the selected security component must be integrated programmatically into the system, the selection of a security component may best be addressed at the requirement stage because subsequent risk assessment and security pattern selection may be affected by this decision. Security pattern repositories, such as [26], and pattern classification and categorization methods, such as [27], can be useful during the pattern selection and identification process.

4.2   Design Stage

Of course, not all security patterns can be identified as early as the requirement stage. Security patterns may be identified during the design stage to leverage some design constraints. Furthermore, some of the security patterns selected at the previous stage may not adhere to the proposed architecture of the system. Hence, a refinement selection activity should be expected at this stage to resolve such issues.

The SAFECode documentation [10] suggests that every security pattern reveals a solution that "consists of a set of interacting roles that can be arranged into multiple concrete design structures". If the structures of security patterns are aligned with the other design structures of the system, an architectural integration between all the structural components and their interrelationships is produced.

Although many security design pattern studies have been published, as described in section 2.2, the Open Group presented a very coherent design methodology to improve security [28]. This technical report proposed the use of three generative sequences (one main and two sub-sequences) for applying security patterns during the design stage. The main sequence is the System Security Sequence and the sub-sequences are the Available System Sequence and the Protected System Sequence [28].

4.3   Implementation Stage

In this stage, the security rules produced during the design phase are coded based on the secure coding best practice. The selected security components are integrated with the corresponding system components according to the architectural design. No security patterns exist specifically for this stage [20]. However, many secure development methodologies can use published attack patterns as a security education tool and sometimes as test case drivers.

Also, rigorous threat-based testing for structural components of the pre-selected patterns is fundamental in this stage. Thus, the ISDF anticipates the adherence to the best practices of coding and testing mandated by the secure development lifecycle in the coding and testing phases, respectively.

4.4   Post Implementation Stage

This stage corresponds to the last two stages of the secure software development lifecycle in the ISDF, namely deployment and operation. The transition between deployment and operation always raises a critical security concern; carrying the integrity and authenticity of the software source code throughout its chain of custody. The code integrity and handling practice during the deployment phase addresses this concern. However, we strongly believe that there is a need for a new security pattern to effectively safeguard this transition in parallel with the above mentioned practice.

After the software is deployed into its operational environment, it is important to monitor responses to flaws and vulnerabilities of the system to check for new evolved patterns. Note that it is important to avoid simply declaring that the individual code batches and bug fixes represent new patterns. Once a new security pattern has been found and documented, then feedback of the new pattern has to go back to the requirement stage for further security improvement in the consequent releases.

During the operational lifetime of the system, it is essential to revisit the requirement and design stages before implementing the new security counter-measures that resulted from new security threats and attacks. In fact, many recent software security vulnerabilities exist because of the lack of a thorough consideration of the countermeasure defenses implemented at the earlier stages.

5   An Example

To better illustrate the advantages of our framework, we use a simple e-commerce system (called eShop) as an example. An e-commerce example is used because of the popularity and clarity of its prime functionalities. The aim is to demonstrate the effectiveness of the interweaving between best practices and security patterns provided by our framework. While it is impossible to present the entire case study due to space limitations, a subset of the case will be presented covering the requirements and design stages described in Section 4.

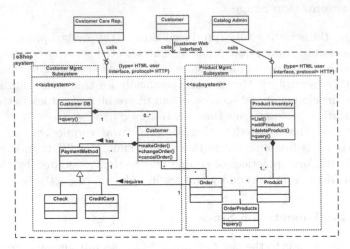

Fig. 2. eShop Preliminary Design

The system, as depicted in Figure 2, has three external (remotely connected) user groups: customers, product catalog administrators, and customer care representatives. Note that, the intent of this diagram is to show some structural components of the eShop system and hence it does not strictly follow the formal UML class diagram notation. The functional requirements of each user group can be summarized as follows.

- *Customers*: browse products and place orders.
- *Product catalog administrators*: remotely manage the product catalog.
- *Customer care representatives*: remotely manage customers' data and orders.
For the non-functional requirements, we focus exclusively on security.

5.1 Stage 1: Requirements

As mentioned earlier, to better employ the strength of the framework, one must work through the best practice activity and the security pattern activity in parallel fashion. The following is a subset of the security requirements of the eShop.

> *Sq1: The system shall enforce authentication of users in a secure manner.*
> *Sq2: The system shall be able to log and trace back all customer transactions.*
> *Sq3: The system shall ensure the privacy and protection of customer data and order transactions.*

These security requirements explicitly impose the need to satisfy some related security properties. The first requirement forces the confidentiality of the access control technique. The second requirement imposes the accountability of customers. The third requirement impresses the confidentiality and integrity of the customer data and transactions. Now that the security properties of the requirements are clear, security patterns can be identified. For the first requirement, **Authentication Enforcer** [29] pattern is selected to handle the problem of how to verify that a subject (customer) is really who they say they are. Next, the accountability property imposes two sub objectives: auditing and non-repudiation [11]. Non-repudiation focuses on capturing evidence so that users who engage in an event cannot later deny that engagement. Auditing refers to the process of monitoring and analyzing logs to report any indication of a security violation. The **Audit Interceptor** [29] is selected to intercept and log requests to satisfy the auditing objective imposed by the second requirement. Finally, the **Secure Pipe** [29] was chosen to fulfill the third requirement and prevent 'man-in-the-middle' attacks. Note that even though the process of identifying the correct patterns is a bit difficult and requires a certain level of security expertise, it can be simplified by consulting an organized security patterns inventory like [26].

5.2 Stage 2: Design

It is expected that not all security patterns can be discovered as early as the requirement stage. In fact, most patterns identified here are a result of architectural design constraints or as a mitigation strategy to identified threats. Thus, the patterns selection refinement process is crucial in this stage.

It is obvious that with multiple entry points to the system (i.e., an entry point for each user group), some of the patterns identified during the requirement stage may need to be replicated (e.g., the authentication mechanism). As shown in Figure 2, three user group entities are interacting with the system at three distinct entry points. However, allowing more entry points may increase the system's risk exposure. For example, a malicious attacker could attempt to impersonate a legitimate user to gain access to his/her resources. This could be particularly serious if the impersonated user has a high level of privilege like a *customer care representative role* or a *product catalog administrator role*. The imposter may then be able to compromise the system and disclose customer credit information. In addition, an intensive threat modeling process must be utilized during this stage to capture the range of potential threats. The design constraints and potential threats identified in this stage collectively influence the refinement process for the preselected patterns. As mentioned above, replicating the authentication mechanism over multiple entry points is problematic and may increase exposure to risks.

One possible solution is to unify the system's entry points into a single point of responsibility. This simplifies the control flow since everything must go through a **Single Access Point** [14]. Figure 3 depicts a refinement of the selected patterns integrated into the eShop architectural design. As an abstraction to simplify the design, we encapsulated the eShop internal entities in a single entity called *eShop inner components*.

Along with the **Single Access Point**, access requests must be validated and authenticated by some type of **Check Point** [11]. A **Check Point** establishes a critical section where security must be enforced through a security policy

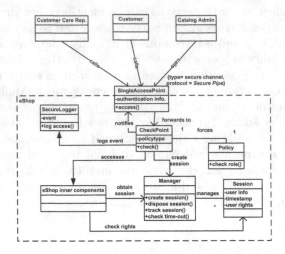

Fig. 3. eShop Integrated Security Patterns

that incorporates different organizational security policies. In terms of the eShop system, the `Check Point` receives a request from the `Single Access Point` and provides validation for a user's options within the restrictions of group policy. Then, the `Check Point` uses a `Secure Logger` [29] to log the event in a secure manner. If access is granted, the `Check Point` then instantiates a `Session` [29] object for the user. The `Session` object holds those security variables associated with the user that may be needed by other components. The `Check Point` uses a *Manager* component to keep track of active session objects. The *eShop inner components* entity authorizes the user by asking the *Manager* for the underlying session object and checking the user's data stored there.

Finally, access to sensitive resources (such as *product inventory* and *customer DB*) may require additional authentication. Therefore, an `Authenticator` [11] can be used to further verify the identity of the subject prior to granting access to these resources. This places an extra, yet important, defensive shield against malicious attacks like those described earlier. However, the `Authenticator` is not shown in Figure 3 due to simplification reasons.

6   Conclusion and Future Work

Our work proposes an integrated framework for developing secure software based on the combination of secure development best practices and security patterns. We also present a four-stage development engineering process to better utilize security patterns with software secure development methodologies. Furthermore, we illustrated how the ISDF framework can be utilized to build more secure software.

Our framework yields two main contributions toward efforts to advance the engineering process to construct more secure software. First, the ISDF framework uniquely consolidates the security patterns with software development best practices. Combining the two will not only simplify the process of building more secure software, but also reduce the risks associated with using ad-hoc security approaches in software development. Second, the ISDF framework enables developers with limited security experience to more easily and more reliably develop secure software.

Our approach also helps to resolve two issues noted in the security patterns literature. The first is the observation that 35 percent of the published patterns do not pass the soundness test for patterns and, therefore, are considered to be guidelines or principals and not formal patterns [15]. For example, security patterns like **Asset Valuation** and **Threat Assessment** [11] don't conform to the formal definition of a security pattern [15,20]. However, since the ISDF incorporates best practices to guide secure development, there is no need to utilize those types of pattern.

The second issue is the lack of patterns for some parts of the development phase (e.g., the small number of attack patterns for use in the design phase) [20]. Our framework resolves this limitation by mandating concrete best practices in parallel with security patterns.

In the future, we will continue to work towards the formalization of the ISDF framework and the discovery of security metrics that can be measured at early stages of the development lifecycle. Also, we will investigate the reversibility of the framework on a legacy system.

Acknowledgment

We would like to thank the Institute of Public Administration (IPA)in Saudi Arabia for their support to this work.

References

1. Viega, J., McGraw, G.: Building Secure Software. Addison-Wesley, Reading (2002)
2. Davis, N., Humphrey Jr., W., Zibulski, S.R., McGraw, G.: Processes for producing secure software. IEEE Security & Privacy 2(3), 18–25 (2004)
3. Howard, M.: Building more secure software with improved development process. IEEE Security & Privacy 2(6), 63–65 (2004)
4. Jayaram, K.R., Mathur, A.: Software engineering for secure software- state of the art: A survey. Technical report, Purdue University (2005)
5. Alkussayer, A., Allen, W.H.: Towards secure software development: Integrating security patterns into a secure SDLC. In: The 47th ACM Southeast Conference (2009)
6. Howard, M., Lipner, S.: The Security Development Lifecycle SDL: A Process for Developing Demonstrably More Secure Software. Microsoft Press (2006)
7. McGraw, G.: Software Security: Building Security. Addison-Wesley, Reading (2006)
8. Howard, M., Lipner, S.: Inside the windows security push. IEEE Security & Privacy 1(1), 57–61 (2003)
9. McGraw, G.: Software security. IEEE Security & Privacy 2(2), 80–83 (2004)

10. Simpson, S.: Fundamental practices for secure software development: A guide to the most effective secure development practices in use today (2008), `http://www.safecode.org`

11. Schumacher, M., Frenandez-Buglioni, E., Hybertson, D., Buschmann, F., Sommerlad, P.: Security Patterns: Integrating Security and Systems Engineering. John Wiley & Sons, Chichester (2006)

12. Alexander, C., Ishikawa, S., Jacobson, M., Fiksdahl-King, I., Angel, S.: A Pattern Language: Towns, Buildings, Construction. Oxford University Press, Oxford (1977)

13. Gamma, E., Helm, R., Johnson, R., Vlissides, J.: Design Patterns: Elements of Reusable Object-Oriented Software. Addison- Wesley Professional (1995)

14. Yoder, J., Barcalow, J.: Architecural patterns for enabling application security. In: PLoP 1997 Conference (1997)

15. Heyman, T., Yskout, K., Scandariato, R., Joosen, W.: An analysis of the security patterns landscape. In: 3rd International Workshop on Software Engineering for Secure Systems (2007)

16. Fernandez, E.B., Pan, R.: A pattern language for security models. In: PLoP 2001 Conference (2001)

17. Hatebur, D., Heisel, M., Schmidt, H.: Security engineering using problem frames. In: International Conference on Emerging Trends in Information and Communication Security (ETRICS) (2006)

18. Horvath, V., Dorges, T.: From security patterns to implementation using petri nets. In: International Conference on Software Engineering (2008)

19. Supaporn, K., Prompoon, N., Rojkangsadan, T.: An approach: Constructing the grammar from security patterns. In: 4th International Joint Conference on Computer Science and Software Engineering (JCSSE 2007) (2007)

20. Yoshioka, N., Washizaki, H., Maruyama, K.: A survey on security patterns. Progress in Informatics (5), 35–47 (2008)

21. Aprville, A., Pourzandi, M.: Secure software development by example. IEEE Security & Privacy 3(4), 10–17 (2005)

22. Jurjens, J.: Secure System Development with UML. Springer, Heidelberg (2004)

23. Valenzuela, I.: Integration ISO17799 into your software development lifecycle. Secure 11, 29–36 (2007)

24. Fernandez, E.B.: A methodology for secure software design. In: International Conference on Software Engineering Research and Practice (2004)

25. Fernandez, E.B., Yoshioka, N., Washizaki, H., Jurjens, J.: Using security patterns to build secure systems. In: 1st International Workshop on Software Patterns and Quality (SPAQu 2007) (2007)

26. Yskout, K., Heyman, T., Scandariato, R., Joosen, W.: An inventory of security patterns. Technical report, Katholieke Univerity Leuven, Department of Computer Science (2006)

27. Hafiz, M., Adamczyk, P., Johnson, R.E.: An organizing security patterns. IEEE Software 24(4), 52–60 (2007)

28. Blakley, B., Heath, C.: of the Open Group Security Forum, M.: Security design patterns. Technical report, Open Group (2004)

29. Steel, C., Nagappan, R., Lai, R.: Core Security Patterns: Best Practices and Strategies forJ2EE, Web Services, and Identity Managment. Prentice-Hall, Englewood Cliffs (2005)

Client Hardware-Token Based Single Sign-On over Several Servers without Trusted Online Third Party Server

Sandro Wefel and Paul Molitor

Institute for Computer Science
Martin-Luther-University Halle-Wittenberg
06099 Halle, Germany
{sandro.wefel,paul.molitor}@informatik.uni-halle.de

Abstract. User authentication in most systems is done by the principle: registration with unique user name and presentation of a secret, e. g., a password or a private cryptographic key, respectively. To obtain a trustworthy method, combinations of hardware token with user certificates and keys secured by a PIN have to be applied.

The main problem of hardware tokens is consumer acceptance. Thus, hardware tokens have to be provided with added values.

This paper proposes such an add-on, namely a client-based approach which allows single sign-on for multiple client applications possibly distributed over several servers without modifications on server side. Whereas current client based hardware token approaches store passwords for authenticating the user to the applications, the approach presented here uses the user certificate stored in the token. A method is provided so that the PIN of the token has to be put in only once and not each time an application is called. Authorization information is taken from a central data base. Thus, the value added to the hardware token consists of both a much more secure authentication method than authentication by user name and secret and single sign-on. So the increase of the consumer acceptance comes along with more security: a win-win situation.

1 Introduction

One main drawback of password authentication is the fact that many users use one and only one easy to keep in mind password for authentication in all their environments. Therefore other authentication methods which are more secure have to be adopted.

Smartcards and other forms of hardware tokens allow the user to keep information, e. g., private keys and passwords, in safe custody. They are especially suitable for being used in the context of public key systems when provided with interfaces to call methods requiring vital information. Such hardware tokens ensure that the private keys never leave the token under any circumstances and thus enhance reliability to a large extent. A user has to authenticate himself to

J.H. Park et al. (Eds.): ISA 2009, CCIS 36, pp. 29–36, 2009.
© Springer-Verlag Berlin Heidelberg 2009

the token. He shows his legitimation by sending a biometrical or a secret information to the token. This process of authentication to the hardware token is called *Card-Holder-Verification* (CHV), a notion originating from smartcards.

After authentication of the user to the token, the token offers methods to read protected information or to use signature or other cryptographic operations for different purposes. In particular these cryptographic operations can be used for certificate based authentication of the token owner. These operations can be executed by the processor which is integrated on the token once authentication to the hardware token has succeeded. Accordingly, it is ensured that one of the criteria for user authentication, the ownership factor, cannot be duplicated. Thus, misuse of legitimation information is hard when stored in hardware tokens. Protection against a misuse after token loss should be given by CHV. If CHV is done by PIN input, the PIN has to be secured in the manner a password is secured.

Certificate based authentication in combination with hardware token solves the initial mentioned problem of inadequate passwords. Section 2 demonstrates that for standard software applications client certificate authentication is possible already now. The problem however is that usually an easy number combination is chosen as PIN by the user if the PIN has to be put in very often during a session, e. g., for each application he calls. So an attacker who plans to steal the token can easily obtain the PIN by glimpsing at its input. Thus, the number of PIN inputs should be reduced for enhancing reliability, as in this case there is hope that the consumer chooses a more hard number combination as PIN. Furthermore lowering the number of times the PIN has to be put in also leads to a better consumer acceptance of using hardware tokens – it leads us to single sign-on. In Section 3 we present a practical approach in which the PIN has to be entered only once, namely during the login to the operation system. This approach works on client side and does not need to modify server software or the interconnection between the servers, if the server allows certificate based authentication.

2   Hardware Token Authentication

Hardware tokens can be applied for authentication to local services, i. e., services located on the local computer, and to network applications. Since the implementation of the RSA Security Inc. PKCS#11 Cryptographic Token Interface [1] neither extra software nor special tokens for the different types of applications are necessary. PKCS#11 is a standard which specifies an *application programming interface* (API), called *Cryptoki*, to devices which hold cryptographic information and perform cryptographic functions. It addresses the goals of technology independence (any kind of device) and resource sharing (multiple applications accessing multiple devices), presenting to applications a common, logical view of the hardware token.

Fig. 1 shows the common use of an hardware token. Several applications access the token by the PKCS#11 interface, provided by a computer library

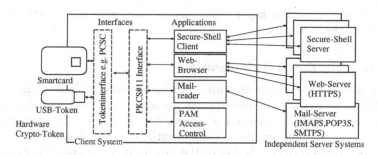

Fig. 1. Standard usage of crypto hardware token in applications

of the token manufacturer. The PKCS#11 interface accesses the token via a hardware interface, e. g., a smartcard reader or an USB connector.

For an all-purpose hardware token based authentication in typically network environments supply of the required certificates and application specific private keys methods have to be provided by the token. We are looking for an approach which operates without using different certificates for different applications. To attack this problem, we have met the challenge of implementing a usable and practicable solution for a representative set of software services. The services so chosen should cover the most needed requirements for authentication in daily routine: restricted access to web services via web browsers, fetch and submit emails, secure terminal applications (Secure Shell) and of course user login to the operating system.

While Secure Shell has its own protocol, the first two applications mentioned above can use SSL/TLS secure communication channels which offers certificate authentication too. In the following subsections, we take a more detailed look at authentication in those different settings.

2.1   Certificate Based User Authentication

A token has to provide methods allowing the token owner to prove that he is the person he pretends to be. A token may hold X.509 certificates [2] beside the private key. Such a certificate certifies the affiliation of the token owner, described by a unique item, to the public key [3]. For a certificate based authentication the presented certificate is checked. If the check holds, a challenge has to be responded by using the associated private key in order to finish successfully the authentication process. There are several network and application protocols which can be used.

Many applications, which require a secured transport channel, use the "SSL Protocol Version 3.0" or its extension described in the "TLS Protocol Version 1.0". In these protocols, which work in the application layer of the OSI reference model, only the presence of the server certificate is necessarily required. However, the protocol offers the possibility to ask for and check the client certificate, too [4]. This allows an user to authenticate to the server. The secure shell (SSH) provides different types of user authentication [5]. Public key authentication methods belong to them. The public key, required for this authentication method, can be obtained from the certificate.

2.2 Certificate Based Authorization

Applications using passwords or similar methods often combine authentication with authorization – only authorized users possess username-password combinations. User certificates are however used only for authentication. Authorization has to be done by another method after authentication has succeeded. This drawback of user certificates is due to the fact that a user holds only one certificate in general, but can have different roles with respect to the application. As different roles cannot be handled by the same certificate other methods for authorization in addition to hardware token authentication have to be provided by the system. Thus, authentication cannot directly imply authorization. The certificate should describe a unique user. For this purpose, in addition to the authentication step further authorization steps are required where the information from the user certificate may be used [6]. The most adequate approach is to use a central or a local LDAP server. The information gathered from the certificate or the certificate itself could be used for the LDAP request.

2.3 A Working Infrastructure

As described in the previous section, authentication using certificates should not automatically lead to the authorization of the users with respect to an application, in general. For this reason we focus only on solutions which allow to combine certificate based authentication and user authorization by using the certificates for retrieving authorization information from central databases.

Restricted access to web services: The most common client applications accessing a web service are web browsers. Most of them allow password authentication methods. A disadvantage of password authentication is the required transmission of the password from the client to the server. To avoid clear text password transmission digest authentication methods should be applied. However, not all client and server applications do support this kind of authentication methods. For this reason, most servers communicate with the clients over channels secured by SSL/TLS during the authentication. Such a channel allows SSL/TLS client authentication as already described in Sect. 2.1, so that user authentication can be installed at this point.

Fetch and submit emails: The SMTP (Simple Mail Transfer Protocol) [7] describes the electronic mail transport from one user to the mailbox of another user. Reading received emails is carried out by calling a web service which accesses the corresponding mailbox, in general. To fetch received emails from the mailbox stored on a server to the client computer, POP3 or IMAP protocols are used [8,9]. Both allow connections using secured channels. User identification could be done by using SMTP-AUTH which extends SMTP to include an authentication step. However, if the first SMTP server also allows identification of a legitimate user by certificate based authentication, a hardware token can be used for authentication [10]. Unlike mail transport both protocols for fetching emails, POP3 and IMAP, require the unique identification of the user [9]. But POP3 and IMAP explicitly provide secured channels using SSL/TLS [11], however not for authentication purposes. Nevertheless there are email mailbox systems which allow SSL/TLS certificate based authentication. The certificate allows extraction of data allowing the mapping of the users to their mailboxes by means of a central user database.

Secure terminal applications, secure shell: Most server and client SSH applications allow public key authentication. By slight extensions most of these client applications can access hardware tokens to obtain the user keys. In order to allow certificate based authentication, OpenSSH has to be extended so that the user public key is obtained from the user certificate and the server checks the authorization by the presented certificate data instead of comparing the user public key with a stored bunch of allowed public keys. There are some suitable patches [12] which can be used for this purpose. In particular, they allow the servers to obtain certificates and certificate revocation lists from a central database, e. g., an LDAP server. Thus, OpenSSH can use the same mechanisms for certificate check as SSL/TLS does which reduces administration efforts.

Local authentication to the operating system: The mechanisms to log in to the operating system by means of hardware token with a user certificate highly depend on the operating system used. Most operating systems allow the usage of a Pluggable Authentication Modules (PAM) to log in and for other authentication purposes, e. g., to turn-off a screensaver. The PKCS#11 PAM Login Tools offers a module which can be used for authentication to hardware token with the PKCS#11 interface.

There currently exist applications for each of the protocols we have discussed in this section which allow certificate based authentication with hardware token and the storage of authorization information in a central database. This leads to a system which works in the manner shown in Fig. 1.

3   Single-Sign-On

As already mentioned in Sect. 2, one of the mostly used standards for token access is the PKCS#11 specification with Cryptoki as API. This software interface hides hardware details to a large extent.

To access private objects stored on a hardware token, an application which uses Cryptoki has to be firstly authenticated to the token by asking the user for a PIN. Thus the user has to put in his PIN every time an application is called. This may be a nuisance. To avoid multiple inputs of a PIN by one and the same user, each user has to be encapsulated in a user session during the login to the operating system. That way separated from other users, each user has to put in his PIN only once during a session. After acceptance of the PIN, the hardware token can be used by every application of the said user session without calling back the user. In the following, we discuss in detail such a token based *Single-Sign-On* (SSO) approach.

There already exist vendor specific multiapplication SSO solutions in combination with hardware token, which use the token as password safe. Our approach targets SSO as combination from vendor independent hardware token and the more secure certificate based user authentication instead of password authentication.

Let us review in detail how Cryptoki is commonly used by an application: (a) The PKCS#11 library is opened and tokens are searched for by scanning the appropriate slots. (b) An application session to the token is started which allows the application for reading the public objects of the token. (c) The user has to be authenticated to the token before the application may use private objects. After usage (d) the logout procedure is called, and (e) the application session as well as the libraries are closed. To adapt the approach to SSO, steps (c) and (d) are the interesting one. In step (c), the PKCS#11 login procedure C_Login() asks the user for authenticating himself, e. g., by input of the PIN. The login status persists until the C_Logout() procedure is called in step (d). However, even during this time period only the corresponding application session is permitted to use private objects on the token. Each other opened application session requires an extra authentication of the user, even if the application is called by one and the same user. From the perspective of the user the required authentication steps could be reduced, if the PIN is temporary stored during the first authentication step and inserted automatically for following log in of applications running in the same operating system user session. The PIN has to be stored until the last applications logs out from the token or the user logs out from the operating system.

A way to arrive at SSO is to use an agent which stores the PIN, not the passwords like other agents do, and is asked when a process needs to authenticate to the token. Fig. 2 shows our approach which is an extension of the one shown in Fig. 1. We aimed at not having to modify the applications themselves. We only extend the PKCS#11 interface in the local machine.

A transparent layer between the applications and the PKCS#11 interface is introduced. This intermediate layer plays the role of a proxy which connects

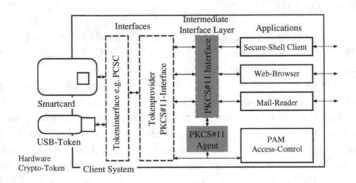

Fig. 2. Token access with SSO-Agent

the applications to the PKCS#11 interface and works in combination with the agent, which stores the user's PIN. Agent functionality is known from the widely used SSH-Agent [13], but in contrast to it, no decrypted secret key is stored in the agent but only the PIN.

First, an user logs into the operating system by authenticating himself. For this purpose, he connects his crypto token with the interface and - in the login screen - enters his PIN. The PAM Access Control gets the PIN and logs into the token, verifies the certificate and starts a challenge to the private key in the token. If the response is correct, the login is successful. During the login process, the PIN passed to the vendor PKCS#11 library is duplicated and stored into the agent. In further steps, the applications do not use the vendor specific PKCS#11 library directly. They connect to the intermediate PKCS#11 library, which offers the same interface as described in [1]. Most interface calls are delegated from the intermediate to the vendor library without modifications. When an application has to authenticate to the token, the agent is asked for the PIN.

To avoid further PIN asking dialogs, the intermediate PKCS#11 library tells all applications with a special flag (CKF_PROTECTED_AUTHENTICATION_PATH) that there is a "protected authentication path", which means, a user can log in to the token without passing a PIN.

We have successfully implemented a system which provides the functionality of the proposed approach. For this purpose we have extended the PAM PKCS#11 library so that the agent is started after a successful login with a given PIN. Among others, Firefox, Thunderbird and OpenSSH have been used as user applications in the test system, which works out-of-the-box.

In combination with our SSO solution we have to ensure that the PIN stored in the system's main memory cannot be used by unauthorized applications. To get this point under control, the system has to check whether the source of the connection is an authorized application when a connection to the interface library is done. Authorized applications could be defined by an administrator using software signatures or checksums as footprint. The agent could check the footprint and ensure that only defined applications are accepted.

Another important item directly concerns the storage of the PIN in the system's main memory. This location has to be protected against malicious attacker programs. To ensure that not a scan of the whole main memory reveals the PIN in clear form, the agent generates a key, encrypts the PIN with this key and decrypts it when necessary. By this, it is rather difficult to get knowledge of the PIN as the key has to be located and extracted, too.

The agent detects the removal of the hardware token. When the token is unplugged, the PIN is deleted from the system's main memory. The memory addresses are overwritten with random values.

Securing the system as described should lead to an SSO environment without (much more) higher security risk than the risk of a system in which the PIN is asked for every time a Cryptoki session is started.

4   Résumé and Conclusions

The approach described in this paper allows to use one and the same personalized hardware token for authentication to several systems. If a PKI exists, the systems themselves do not need to be connected to a central server which undertakes the task of authenticating the users. In fact each system could authenticate a user by using the user's personalized hardware token which is plugged into the system. Above all the different local systems could apply different methods to decide whether a user can be accepted. The authorization information could be stored in a database either located in the local environment or in a central database, e. g., an LDAP server could be used which results in a complete system with local authentication and central user management. The programs of the applications need not to be modified in order to be used in this setting.

The system can be easily upgraded in order to provide SSO without a online central login or ticketing system, which is required by other SSO systems, e. g., kerberos. Modifications to the network clients and server software are minimal, if at all necessary. The patches used are widespread well known regular upgrades. Only the extended token login application which provides the SSO agent is a new system software which has to be installed on the client. This whole SSO system runs on client side and can coexist with other systems.

References

1. RSA Laboratories: PKCS #11: Cryptographic Token Interface Standard (2004), http://www.rsa.com/rsalabs/node.asp?id=2133
2. ITU-T: Recommendation X.509 Information technology - Open Systems Interconnection -The Directory: Authentication framework (1997)
3. Housley, R., Polk, W., Ford, W., Solo, D.: Internet X.509 public key infrastructure certificate and certificate revocation list (CRL) profile. RFC 3280, IETF (April 2002)
4. Thomas, S.A.: SSL and TLS Essentials. Securing the Web. John Wiley & Sons, Chichester (2000)
5. Ylonen, T., Lonvick, C.: The Secure Shell (SSH) Authentication Protocol. RFC 4252 (January 2006)
6. Thompson, M.R., Essiari, A., Mudumbai, S.: Certificate-based Authorization Policy in a PKI Environment. ACM Transactions on Infomation and System Security (August 2003)
7. Klensin, J.: Simple mail transfer protocol. RFC 2821, IETF (April 2001)
8. Myers, J., Rose, M.: Post office protocol - version 3. RFC 1939, IETF (May 1996)
9. Crispin, M.: Internet Message Access Protocol - Version 4rev1. RFC 3501, IETF (March 2003)
10. Hoffman, P.: SMTP service extension for secure SMTP over TLS. RFC 2487, IETF (January 1999)
11. Newman, C.: Using TLS with IMAP, POP3 and ACAP. RFC 2595, IETF (1999)
12. Petrov, R.: X.509v3 certificates for OpenSSH (March 2007), http://roumenpetrov.info/openssh/
13. Barrett, D.J., Silverman, R.E., Byrnes, R.G.: SSH, The Secure Shell: The Definitive Guide, 2nd edn. O'Reilly, Sebastopol (2005)

Concurrency and Time in Role-Based Access Control

Chia-Chu Chiang and Coskun Bayrak

Department of Computer Science,
University of Arkansas at Little Rock,
2801 South University Avenue,
Little Rock, Arkansas 72204-1099, USA
{cxchiang,cxbayrak}@ualr.edu

Abstract. Role-based access control (RBAC) has been proposed as an alternative solution for expressing access control policies. The generalized temporal RBAC (GTRBAC) extends RBAC by adding time in order to support timed based access control policies. However, GTRBAC does not address certain issues of concurrency such as, synchronization. We propose an approach to the expressions of time and concurrency in RBAC based on timed Petri nets. A formal verification method for access control policies is also proposed.

Keywords: Concurrency, GTRBAC, Petri Nets, RBAC, Temporal Logic, Time.

1 Introduction

Traditional role-based access control models that are subject to users and files have their limitations. Role-based access control has been proposed for expressing access control policies [1]. However, several issues still exist in RBAC. Particularly, time and concurrency are not taken into the consideration of design in the traditional RBAC models.

Time and concurrency both play a key role in RBAC for applications that have critical requirements of tasks in managing timed and synchronous access such as role enabling/disabling. Time is an ordering imposed on tasks. Different tasks with different timing can also occur simultaneously. This indeterminacy in the order of tasks can pose serious problems that can creep into RBAC for access control. The root of the problems is that more than one task may be trying to manipulate the shared state at the same time. If this happens, we need to have some way to make sure that RBAC behaves correctly. In addition, RBAC assumes task transitions instantaneous in time that might not be practical in applications where the task transitions might take the duration of time. To address these issues, we are proposing an approach to add constraints on time and allow concurrency in access control policies in RBAC. The timing in RBAC will be expressed and analyzed using timed-based Petri nets.

The expected outcomes of this research will include,

- Allowing access control policies to be expressed in time and concurrency,
- Allowing access control policies to be proved for correctness,

J.H. Park et al. (Eds.): ISA 2009, CCIS 36, pp. 37–42, 2009.

• Allowing access control policies to be modeled in a timed Petri net, and
• Providing a tool for the modeling of behavior of time and concurrency based RBAC.

The remainder of the paper is organized as follows. Section 2 introduces the backgrounds on Petri nets including timing. The traditional RBAC, GTRBAC, and the proposed RBAC for timing and concurrency are defined in Section 3. An example is illustrated to demonstrate the core expressions of time and concurrency in TCRBAC. Section 4 presents the reachability analysis technique to analyze the correctness of events in TCRBAC occurring concurrently and also constrained in timing. Section 5 presents tools support for the simulation of TCRBAC. Finally the paper is summarized in Section 6.

2 Backgrounds on Petri Nets

Petri nets [2] have been widely used to model concurrent systems. The use of Petri nets in RBAC is to verify the consistency of RBAC. The constraints including cardinality, separation of duty, precedence, and dependence can be verified using the Petri net reachability analysis technique. The use of Petri nets in RBAC ensures the consistency of access control policy in RBAC, reducing the vulnerabilities and security risks of the underlying systems. In this section, we briefly review the Petri nets and the graphs.

Definition 1. A Petri net, as a directed bipartite graph, is defined to be a 4-tuple <P, T, I, O>, where

• P is a finite set of places.
• T is a finite set of transitions. P and T are disjoint.
• I: T → P that defines the set of input places for each transition t_i, denoted as $I(t_i)$.
• O: T → P that defines the set of output places for each transition t_i, denoted as $O(t_i)$.

Definition 2. A marked Petri net with the marking μ is a 5-tuple <P, T, I, O, μ>, where

• P, T, I, and O are defined in Petri net.
• μ: P → N that defines the number of tokens in the place P_i and N is the natural numbers.

A Petri net cannot model time, thus several methods have been presented to introduce time in Petri nets [3]. Basically, time is attached to either places or transitions in Petri nets. Merlin and Farber [4] present time in transitions. In [5] and [6], time is presented in paces as waiting time. Once a token is produced in a place, the place will not be enabled until time has elapsed. In general, a timed Petri net (TPN) is defined below,

Definition 3. A timed Petri net is a 5-tuple <P, T, I, O, C>, where

• P, T, I, and O are defined in Petri net.
• C is associated to each transition t_i, denoted as [ti_{min}, ti_{max}] where $0 \le ti_{min} < \infty$ and $0 \le ti_{max} \le \infty$. In addition, $ti_{min} \le ti_{max}$ if $ti_{max} \ne \infty$ or $ti_{min} < ti_{max}$ if $ti_{max} = \infty$.

3   Expressing Time and Concurrency

Since a formal method will be applied to the time and concurrency RBAC model, we start to define the general RBAC model in a mathematical manner.

Definition 4. A RBAC policy is a 6-tuple <U, R, P, UA, PA, ≥), where

- U, R, and P are finite sets of users, roles, and permissions.
- $UA \subseteq U \times R$ is the user-role assignment relation $(u, r) \in UA$.
- $PA \subseteq P \times R$ is the role-permission assignment relation $(p, r) \in PA$.
- $\geq \subseteq R \times R$ is a partial order on the set R of roles which creates a role hierarchy in R.

Timing is not taken into consideration in the general RBAC. Joshi et al. [7] proposed a Generalized Temporal RBAC to extend Definition 1 by adding time to it which is defined into Definition 2.

Definition 5. A GTRBAC policy is a 7-tuple <U, R, P, T, UA, PA, ≥), where

- U, R, P, UA, PA, and ≥ are defined in Definition 1.
- T is a finite set of time.

The GTRBAC supports timing constraints on role enabling/disabling, user-role assignment, role permission assignment, role activation, runtime events, and dependencies of events. GTRBAC provides the expressive power of constraints on timing but less expressive power on concurrency. We propose a general Time-Based Concurrent RBAC (TCRBAC) to support timing and concurrency in access control policies.

Definition 6. A TCRBAC policy is a 8-tuple <U, R, P, T, UA, PA, ≥, δ), where

- U, R, P, T, UA, PA, and ≥ are defined in miniHRBAC.
- δ is a finite set of transitions.

In TCRBAC, time can be associated to UA and PA. In addition, time can be expressed in role enabling/disabling, role activation/deactivation that can be considered as events in TCRBAC. For example, John Doe is assigned a role, STUDENT at time t_0, denoted as role-assigned(JOHN DOE, STUDENT, t_0). The role STUDENT is assigned a permission REGISTER-COURSE at time t_1, denoted as permission-assigned(REGISTER-COURSES, STUDENT, t_1). The role of JOHN DOE can be activated at time t_2 as JOHN DOE is assigned to the role STUDENT. As can be seen from this example, there are obvious time dependencies in RBAC. For instance,

- role-assigned(JOHN DOE, STUDENT, t_0) → can-activate(JOHN DOE, STUDENT, t_1).
- permission-assigned(REGISTER-COURSE, STUDENT, t_2) → can-be-acquired(REGISTER-COURSE, STUDENT, t_3).
- can-activate(JOHN DOE, STUDENT, t_1) ∧ can-be-acquired(REGISTER-COURSE, STUDENT, t_3) → can-acquire(JOHN DOE, REGISTER-COURSE, t_4).

In order to analyze the behaviors of time-based concurrent RBAC, we propose to use a timed Petri net to model the TCRBAC. The timed Petri net corresponding to this scenario is shown in Fig. 1.

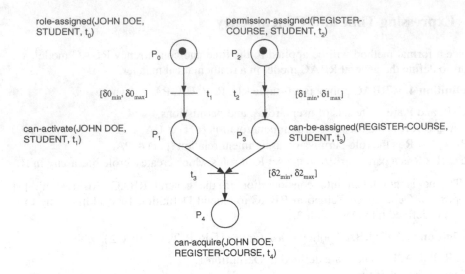

role-assigned(JOHN DOE, STUDENT, t_0)

permission-assigned(REGISTER-COURSE, STUDENT, t_2)

$[\delta0_{min}, \delta0_{max}]$

can-activate(JOHN DOE, STUDENT, t_1)

$[\delta1_{min}, \delta1_{max}]$

can-be-assigned(REGISTER-COURSE, STUDENT, t_3)

$[\delta2_{min}, \delta2_{max}]$

can-acquire(JOHN DOE, REGISTER-COURSE, t_4)

Fig. 1. A corresponding timed petri net

From Fig. 1, the time constraints are shown as follows,

- There is no dependency between P_0 and P_2, thus role-assigned and permission-assigned can occur concurrently. Therefore, there is no relationship between t_0 and t_2.
- t_1 must be in the time interval, $[t_0+\delta0_{min}, t_0+\delta0_{max}]$
- t_3 must be in the time interval, $[t_2+\delta1_{min}, t_2+\delta1_{max}]$
- There is a synchronization point in this graph. P_4 must be enabled as P_1 and P_3 are completed. Neither one is ready, P_4 cannot be enabled. Therefore, t_4 is in the time interval, $[t_0+\delta0_{min}$ or $t_2+\delta1_{min}, t_0+\delta0_{max}$ or $t_2+\delta1_{max}]$. t_4 could be one of the following situations,
  1. If $t_0+\delta0_{min} \leq t_2+\delta1_m$ and $t_0+\delta0_{max} \leq t_2+\delta1_{max}$ then t_4 must be in the time interval $[t_2+\delta1_m, t_2+\delta1_{max}]$.
  2. If $t_0+\delta0_{min} \geq t_2+\delta1_m$ and $t_0+\delta0_{max} \geq t_2+\delta1_{max}$ then t_4 must be in the time interval $[t_0+\delta0_m, t_0+\delta0_{max}]$.
  3. If $t_0+\delta0_{min} \leq t_2+\delta1_m$ and $t_0+\delta0_{max} \geq t_2+\delta1_{max}$ then t_4 must be in the time interval $[t_2+\delta1_m, t_0+\delta0_{max}]$.
  4. If $t_0+\delta0_{min} \geq t_2+\delta1_m$ and $t_0+\delta0_{max} \leq t_2+\delta1_{max}$ then t_4 must be in the time interval $[t_0+\delta0_m, t_2+\delta1_{max}]$.

4   Analysis of TCRBAC

Timed Petri nets are used as a modeling tool of TCRBAC. Places in Petri nets considered as conditions and transitions represent events. Events are concurrent or parallel. Several approaches to the analysis of Timed Petri nets have been used. One commonly used technique is the reachability tree. The tree contains nodes representing markings of the corresponding Petri net and arcs representing the possible changes in state resulting from the firing of transitions. A reachability tree finds a finite representation of a reachability set of a Petri net. The reachability set of a marked Petri net M = <P, T, I, O, C> denoted as R(M) is a set of all states into which the Petri net can enter by any possible execution. The reachability tree of the Petri net depicted in Fig. 2 is shown as follows.

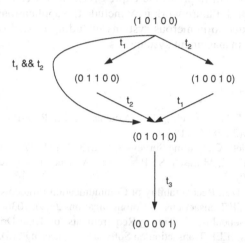

Fig. 2. A corresponding reachability tree of fig. 1

The reachability tree in Fig. 2 is bound and finite. It indicates that John Doe can acquire the registration in either one of the following scenarios,

• t_1 is fired followed by t_2 and t_3,
• t_2 is fired followed by t_1 and t_3,
• t_1 and t_2 are simultaneously fired at the same time, followed by t_3.

The reachability tree can also be primarily used for the analysis of events to occur concurrently with constraints on timing, concurrence, precedence, and frequency of the occurrences.

5 Tools Support

There are several Petri nets tools available in the open resources [8]. Unfortunately, the lack of a standard protocol has forced developers to develop different tools for Petri nets. Several solutions to this problem have been proposed by providing a generic interchange format for Petri nets [9]. Arcoverde et al. [10] developed a tool suite allowing the editing of Petri nets as well as importing/exporting Petri nets from/to different tools. The tool suite allows for Petri nets tools communications for Petri tools integration. We are now evaluating the tools available in [8]. The purpose of this evaluation is to select a free open source tool where we are also able to modify the code for the project. More importantly, this tool must support timing.

6 Summary

Research has been done in introducing time to RBAC but not concurrency. In this paper, we introduced time and concurrency to model the behavior in RBAC. A timed Petri net is used to analyze the time-based RBAC policy. We believe that the addition of time and concurrency will improve the expressiveness power in modeling RBAC behaviors in access control. Future work may include the applications and evaluations of this proposed technique to numerous systems including trusted operating systems and real-time workflow management systems.

References

1. Sandhu, R., Coyne, E.J., Feinstein, H.L., Youman, C.E.: Role-Based Access Control Models. Computer 29(2), 38–47 (1996)
2. Peterson, J.L.: Petri Nets. Computing Surveys 9(3), 223–252 (1977)
3. Ghezzi, C., Mandrioli, D., Morasca, S., Pezze, M.: A General Way to Put Time in Petri Nets, pp. 60–67 (1989)
4. Merlin, P.M., Farber, D.J.: Recoverability of Communication Protocols - Implications of a Theoretical Study. IEEE Transactions on Communications 24(9), 1036–1043 (1976)
5. Coolahan, J.E., Roussopoulos, N.: Timing Requirements for Time Driven Systems using Augmented Petri Nets. IEEE Transaction on Software Engineering 9(5), 603–616 (1983)
6. Stotts Jr., P.D., Pratt, T.W.: Hierarchical Modelling of Software Systems with Timed Petri Nets. In: Proceedings of the 1st International Workshop on Timed Petri Nets, pp. 32–39. IEEE Press, New York (1985)
7. Joshi, J., Bertino, E., Ghafoor, A.: An Analysis of Expressiveness and Design Issues for the Generalized Temporal Role-Based Access Control Model. IEEE Transactions on Dependable and Secure Computing 2(2), 157–175 (2005)
8. Petri Net Tools,
   http://www.informatik.uni-hamburg.de/TGI/PetriNets/tools/
9. Jüngel, M., Kindler, E., Weber, M.: Towards a Generic Interchange Format for Petri Nets,
   http://www.daimi.au.dk/pn2000/Interchange/papers/
   pos_01_final.pdf
10. Arcoverde Jr., A., Alves Jr., G., Lima, R.: Petri Nets Tools Integration through Eclipse. In: Proceedings of the 2005 OOPSLA Workshop on Eclipse Technology Exchange, pp. 90–94. IEEE Press, New York (2005)

Performance Assessment Method
for a Forged Fingerprint Detection Algorithm

Yong Nyuo Shin, In-Kyung Jun, Hyun Kim, and Woochang Shin

Korea Information Security Agency, IT Venture Tower 135, Songpa-gu, Seoul, Korea
{ynshin,ikjeun}@kisa.or.kr, hikim@secutronix.com,
wcshin@skuniv.ac.kr

Abstract. The threat of invasion of privacy and of the illegal appropriation of information both increase with the expansion of the biometrics service environment to open systems. However, while certificates or smart cards can easily be cancelled and reissued if found to be missing, there is no way to recover the unique biometric information of an individual following a security breach. With the recognition that this threat factor may disrupt the large-scale civil service operations approaching implementation, such as electronic ID cards and e-Government systems, many agencies and vendors around the world continue to develop forged fingerprint detection technology, but no objective performance assessment method has, to date, been reported. Therefore, in this paper, we propose a methodology designed to evaluate the objective performance of the forged fingerprint detection technology that is currently attracting a great deal of attention.

Keywords: Forged Fingerprint, Performance Evaluation, Sample Correction, Vitality Test Sample, Recursive Operating Characteristic.

1 Introduction

In the rapidly evolving information society, dysfunction can occur such that personal information is leaked before the information owner realizes it. As a solution, access control technology using biometric characteristics has been proposed. This technology, however, is vulnerable to an attack that utilizes the characteristics of the human body, like a gelatin fingerprints, as noted by a number of studies [1].

With the recognition that this threat factor may disrupt the large-scale civil service operations approaching implementation, such as electronic ID cards and e-Government systems, many agencies and vendors around the world continue to develop forged fingerprint detection technology, but no objective performance assessment method has, to date, been reported. Therefore, this paper proposes a methodology designed to evaluate the objective performance of the forged fingerprint detection technology that is currently attracting a great deal of attention. Following the introduction, chapter 2 outlines existing studies related to our work. Section 3 introduces the performance evaluation procedure. Section 4 describes the biometric sample correction. Section 5 presents the performance evaluator for forged fingerprint detection. The last section provides a conclusion.

J.H. Park et al. (Eds.): ISA 2009, CCIS 36, pp. 43–49, 2009.

2 Related Works

Almost all current forged fingerprint detection systems deploy the forgery detection function at the fingerprint input part with which the system interacts with the user. This has the strength in that a malicious attack is unlikely because an administrator is always monitoring the fingerprint input part at the application area, like at immigration. However, an attack using a forged fingerprint might arise frequently, because an administrator cannot actually watch the process of detecting a forged fingerprint attached to the input part in non face-to-face transactions, like in the online environment.

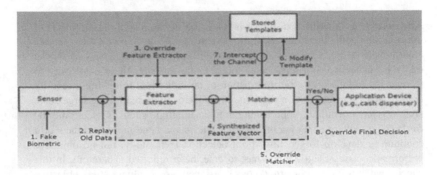

Fig. 1. Analysis of threats in the biometric system

The threats of a general fingerprint recognition system are well analyzed in [2]. As shown in the above figure 1, if we assume that an ideal forged fingerprint detector is loaded on the fingerprint input device, we can expect that a malicious attacker will select the connection between the fingerprint input device and the feature extractor as the attack target. At this time, the attacker can select to re-transmit the authorized user's fingerprint image that has passed through the forged fingerprint detector. Further, the attacker may replace the feature extractor for a feature matcher, or manipulate the data transmitted between each component. However, the response against these manipulation efforts can be defended against using the cryptographic protocol at the end. That is, we can respond to the retransmission of digitalized user features with the challenge and response method or nonce, or by replacing the feature extractor with an introduction of a public key for each device.

3 Performance Evaluation Procedure

It is assumed that an attack made by creating a forged fingerprint would occur only at a fingerprint input device that the attacker faces, based on the premises that an attack detouring an ideal forged fingerprint detector can be effectively blocked. This also holds true if the detector, which determines fingerprint forgery using the signal obtained from the fingerprint input device, exists in feature extractors or feature matchers. Therefore, this paper limits the scope to cases where an attack using a forged fingerprint occurs at the fingerprint input device, and attempts to assess performance by implementing the sample extractor and performance evaluator, composed as following Figure 2.

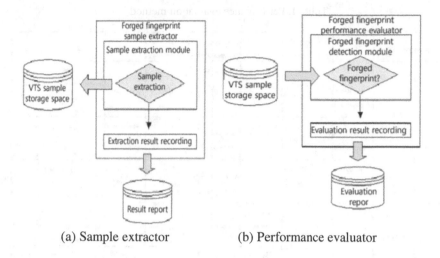

(a) Sample extractor   (b) Performance evaluator

Fig. 2. Configuration of the performance assessment system

3.1 Evaluation Target and Evaluation Method Selection

To perform evaluation performance, the evaluation target should be selected first, and related data should be obtained. The equipment and algorithm to be evaluated should provide a sample extraction module or forged fingerprint detection module as the form of hardware or software. Depending on the evaluation objectives, only the audio and visual I/O are provided through a device like LCD and voice, or detailed outputs relating to each process can be provided in the performance evaluation recording device through a separate interface. However, empirical data has shown that various types of mistakes can occur depending on the degree of fatigue, if the observer should record the audio and visual I/O. There is also the problem whereby the same evaluation result cannot be reproduced.

This paper modifies and applies the three existing performance evaluation methods [3], as shown in the table 1. The first is the technology test that builds up a database for evaluation with the signal showing forged fingerprint status from the forged fingerprint identification equipment, according to a method that is carefully designed in advance. Perform evaluation is then conducted. The second is the scenario test that performs the evaluation after building the online or evaluation database in the system environment, which is designed to fit into the objectives. However, when built up as the evaluation database, the designated forged fingerprint status can be erroneously stored by the system. Therefore, it requires modification. Lastly, the operational test performs an evaluation online or after storage in the actual use environment. In this case, expertise is required to modify the forged fingerprint status that is marked in the database for evaluation.

Table 1. Performance evaluation method

Evaluation type	Target	Environmental design	Sample extraction	Result observation	Evaluation reproducibility	Reliability	Remarks
Existing Test Method	Technical Test	General-purpose equipment	Evaluation agency	Evaluation agency	Evaluation agency	No	Medium	Performance difference and environment inconsistency depending on the selected equipment
	Scenario Based Test	Vendor designation	Using agency	--	Evaluation agency	No	Medium	Observer's degree of fatigue. Unable to reproduce.
	Operational Test	Vendor designation	Using agency	--	Evaluation agency	No	Medium	Observer's degree of fatigue. Unable to reproduce.
Forged fingerprint detection	Technical, Scenario Based, Operational Test	Vendor designation	Developing company	Evaluation agency	Evaluation agency	Yes	High	Reflects the technique characteristics of the development company.
				Developing company	Evaluation agency	Yes	Low	Possibility of false data in the sample.
			Using agency	Evaluation agency	Evaluation agency	Yes	High	Needs to comply with sample storage API.
				Developing company	Evaluation agency	Yes	Low	Possibility of false data in the sample.

3.2 Selecting the Test Sample and Environment

When the evaluation applicant submits the evaluation objects, the population for evaluation should be newly selected or the selected population should be used again. Here, test sample selection refers to the type of signal used by the evaluation target selected by the evaluator to detect the forged fingerprint, determining the number of users to collect biometric information from for evaluation, and the number of samples (use times) to collect. Generally, a fingerprint recognition system is likely to depend on the physical environment conditions of the location where the fingerprint recognition system is installed. It is desirable for the test environment to be selected in advance. The test environments that may be selected such as indoor, outdoor and entryway which able to block rain and sunlight.

4 Sample Correction

The types of signals used to detect the forged fingerprint are diverse, as outlined in a master's thesis written by Marie Sandstrom, from Linkoping University in Sweden. This paper developed the VTS (Vitality Test Sample) and VTD (Vitality Test Data) formats for sample extraction, in order to support access/proximity detection, contact time detection, and the Oxymeter, which is the first dimension row used by the forged fingerprint detection module, as well as the fingerprint and color finger image, which is the second dimension signal row. The following figure shows the composition.

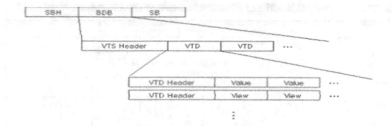

Fig. 3. VTS and VTD composition

In the above figure 3, SBH (Standard Biometric Header), BDB (Biometric Data Block), and SB (Signature Block) are the common data element groups in CBEFF[4], and VTS can be included as the VTS. The VTS is composed of the VTD, linked in random order. Other information that is useful for an analysis of forged fingerprint detection performance can be saved in the VTS's extended data block. The following table 2 shows the case of the first dimension signal in the VTS and VTD structures.

Table 2. VTS structure

Filed	Size	Valid values	Remarks
Format identifier	4 bytes	('V' 'T' 'S' 0x0)	"VTS" - Vitality Test Sample
Version number	4 bytes	('0' '1' '0' 0x0)	"010" - Version 1.0
Record length in bytes	4 bytes	= 16 + The sum of the sizes of all signals	
Vitality type	1 byte	-1, 0, 1	1: Live 0: Forgery -1: Unknown
Number of signal types	2 bytes	>= 1	
Reserved byte	1 byte	00	0 for this version of the standard
Vitality test data			VTD
Extended Data Block Length	2 bytes	0 or >=3	0 = No extended data, Optional, Testing environment info, etc.
Extended Data Area Type Code	2 bytes		Only present if Extended Data Block Length ! = 0
Extended Data	In prev. field		Only present if Extended Data Block Length ! = 0

5   Performance Evaluator for Forged Fingerprint Detection

When the VTS data for evaluation is configured through the sample extraction process, a part of the database is distributed to the person to be evaluated for tuning purposes. Then, the person to be evaluated submits the forged fingerprint determination module that calculates the fingerprint forgery status as a negative value like -1 or a value between 0 and 1 using this data (1 = genuine, 0 = forgery, -1 = unable to determine, other negative numbers = error code). Thereafter, the evaluator performs the performance evaluation using the performance evaluator developed for this paper, as shown below figure 4.

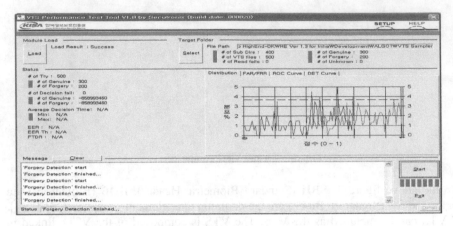

Fig. 4. Performance evaluator

In the figure 4, we can see that the performance of the forged fingerprint detector is displayed by the score distribution, because this paper uses Type 1 and Type 2 errors for the recognition performance evaluation of the current fingerprint recognition algorithm in order to evaluate forged fingerprint detection performance. The incorrect detection of a normal fingerprint as a forged fingerprint is deemed a FRR (False Reject Error) Type 1. On the other hand, if the forged fingerprint is incorrectly determined as a normal one, it is calculated as a FAE (False Accept Error) Type 2. Accordingly, the FNMR (False Non-Match Rate) can be explained by the following expression. The FNMR is the ratio of the number of times that shows the decision score (DS) under the threshold value (t), plus the number of determination failures (N_{FTD}) and the number of failure times (N_{FTA}) against the number of genuine fingerprint attempt times (NG) using a normal fingerprint.

$$FNMR(t) = \frac{card\{DS : DS < t\} + N_{FTD} + N_{FTA}}{NG}$$

The FMR (False Match Rate) is the ratio of the number of times that shows the determination score (DS) under the threshold value (t) against an attack using a forged fingerprint (NF) using a forged fingerprint.

$$FAR(t) = \frac{card\{DS : DS \geq t\}}{NF}$$

Therefore, the result of this paper proves that forged fingerprint performance evaluation can apply all indices equally. These include ROC (Recursive Operating Characteristic) and DET (Detection Error Trade-off), used in a performance evaluation of the current recognition algorithm.

6 Conclusion

This paper finds that technology, the scenario-based, and the operation evaluation method used for recognition performance evaluation of a fingerprint recognition system can be used for performance evaluation of a forged fingerprint without modification. However, technology evaluation was modified before application, meaning samples can be collected using equipment submitted by the person to be evaluated in order to resolve the problem whereby the performance evaluation result is disputed because samples collected from general-purpose equipment selected by the evaluator was forced to the person to be evaluated.

In addition, the VTS data specification was set for sample extraction, so that scenario and operation evaluation results can be reproduced. The company was allowed to present the VTD, which is a component of the VTS, or keep it as a secret, and evaluation result reliability was applied with differentiation.

Additionally, the person to be evaluated was permitted to request performance evaluation after developing the forged fingerprint detector only using the VTS sample collected by the evaluation agency. Also, indexes such as ROC and DET can be utilized. These were developed so as to evaluate the performance of the existing recognition algorithm as a performance evaluation item for the forged fingerprint detector.

References

1. Matsumoto, T., Matsumoto, H., Yamada, K., Hoshino, S.: Impact of artificial gummy fingers on fingerprint systems. In: Proc. SPIE, vol. 4677, pp. 275–289 (2002)
2. Ratha, N.K., Connell, J.H., Bolle, R.M.: Enhancing security and privacy in biometrics-based authentication systems. IBM Systems Journal 40(3), 614–634 (2001)
3. Biometrics Working Group, Best practices in testing and reporting performance of biometric devices, http://www.afb.org.uk/bwg/bestprac10.pdf
4. Sandstrom, M.: Liveness detection in fingerprint recognition systems, LITH-ISY-EX-3557-2004, Linköping University, Sweden (2004)

An Efficient Password Authenticated Key Exchange Protocol with Bilinear Parings[*]

Xiaofei Ding, Fushan Wei, Chuangui Ma, and Shumin Chen

Department of Applied Mathematics,
Zhengzhou Information Science and Technology Institute,
450002, Zhengzhou, China
xiaofei2812@163.com, chuanguima@sina.com, weifs831020@163.com

Abstract. In recent years, many password authenticated key exchange (PAKE) protocols have been proposed. However, many of them have been broken or have no security proof. In this paper, we propose an efficient password authenticated key exchange protocol using bilinear pairings. Compared with previous PAKE protocol using bilinear pairings, our protocol is quite efficient both in communication cost and computational cost. Moreover, this paper proves that the novel protocol is forward secrecy under the Bilinear Diffie-Hellman (BDH) assumption in the random oracle model.

Keywords: PAKE, bilinear paring, BDH, forward secrecy.

1 Introduction

With the increasing popularity of wide-area networks, the problem of insuring privacy and security of data is becoming increasingly important. In order to securely identify remote users and communicate with each other in the insecure network, many schemes have been proposed in the literature. Among these schemes, the password authenticated key exchange (PAKE) protocols [1],[2],[3] are probably the best-accepted and most widely-used schemes because of its easy-to-memorize property.

Das et al.[3] proposed a remote user authentication scheme using bilinear pairings in 2006. In this scheme, they use Timestamps to avoid replay attacks while sending the authentication request over a public channel. In addition, they claimed that the proposed scheme is secure against the forgery attack and the insider attack. But Goriparthi et al. [4] pointed out the replay attack and the forgery attack for Das's scheme. Recently, Juang et al.[6] also found that Das's scheme is easily vulnerable to the offline dictionary attack and replay attack. Until now, most of this kind of schemes lacked many nice properties, such as, identity protection, mutual authentication and session key agreement.

In this paper, we use bilinear pairings to propose an efficient password authenticated key agreement (PAKE) protocol. Then we also prove the novel protocol is

---

[*] This work was partially supported by hi-tech research and development program of China (2007AA01Z431).

J.H. Park et al. (Eds.): ISA 2009, CCIS 36, pp. 50–56, 2009.

secure under the Bilinear Diffie-Hellman assumption in the random oracle model. Furthermore, our protocol is quite efficient both in computational cost and communication cost.

The remainder of this paper is organized as follows. In section 2, we review the related building techniques. In section 3, we recall the communication model and some security definitions of PAKE protocols. Then we propose a novel PAKE protocol using bilinear pairings and give the security proof of the protocol in the random oracle model and compare the efficiency and security of the improved protocol with other protocols in section 4. Finally, we conclude this paper in Section 5.

2 Preliminaries

For convenience, the notations and definitions used in this paper are shown in Table 1.

Table 1. Notations and Definitions

Notation	Definition	Notation	Definition
C, S	Client and Server	$G_1 = \langle P \rangle$	additive cyclic group of order q
pw	Password of C and S	G_2	multiplicative cyclic group
H_i	Hash function	Q	Random element of G_1
s	secret key of S	P_s	public key of S
D	Password space	N	Size of D
ID_C, ID_S	identification of C and S	$\mathcal{A}$	Adversary

Let G_1 be an additive cyclic group of prime order q and G_2 be the multiplicative cyclic group of the same order. Let $\hat{e} : G_1 \times G_1 \rightarrow G_2$ be a bilinear pairing map.

BDH assumption: Let $\mathcal{A}_{bdh}$ be a BDH adversary running in polynomial time t. Consider the experiment: $Exp_{\mathcal{A}_{bdh}}(k) : u, v, w \in_R \mathbb{Z}_q^*$, $U = uP, V = vP, W = wP$; $Z \leftarrow \mathcal{A}_{bdh}(U, V, W)$, if $Z = \hat{e}(P, P)^{uvw}$, $Exp_{\mathcal{A}_{bdh}}(k)$ returns 1, else returns 0. We define the advantage in solving BDH problem as $Adv_{\mathcal{A}_{bdh}}(t, k) = \Pr[Exp_{\mathcal{A}_{bdh}}] = 1$.

The BDH assumption is that the advantage of any adversary $\mathcal{A}_{bdh}$ is negligible.

3 Security Model

In this section, we present the security model we will use in the rest of the paper. The model described in this section is based on that of [7], [8]. In this model, the players do not deviate from the protocol and the adversary is not a player, but does control all the network communications.

3.1 Communicational Model

In a PAKE protocol, there are two types of participants: client C and server S. The client and server share a low-entropy secret pw which is chosen from a small dictionary D of size N. We denote client instances and server instances by C^i and S^j (or by U when we consider any kind of instances). In the model, it is assumed that an adversary can control all communications in the network. During the execution of the protocol, the interaction between an adversary and the protocol participants occurs only via oracle queries, which model the adversary capabilities in a real attack.

These queries from adversary are as follows:

Execute (C^i, S^j)**:** In this query, the adversary can get access to honest executions of P between C^i and S^j by eavesdropping.

Send (U^k, m)**:** This query models an active attack. The adversary gets the response that the participant instance U^k would generate upon receipt of the message m according to the protocol.

Reveal (U^k)**:** This query models the misuse of session keys by instance U^k. It returns to the adversary the session key of instance U, if the latter is defined.

Corrupt (U^k)**:** This query models the possibility of subverting a principal. It returns to the adversary the password of the client instance U^k.

3.2 Security Notions

Freshness: An instance is said to be Fresh in the current protocol execution if the instance has accepted and not been asked Corrupt query, neither it nor the other instance with the same session tag have been asked for a Reveal query.

Test (U^k)**:** This query is used to measure the semantic security of the session key of challenge instance U^k, if the latter is defined. If the key is not defined, it returns $\perp$. Otherwise, it returns either the session key held by instance U^k if $b=0$ or a random of key the same size if $b=1$. This query can be asked at most once by the adversary $\mathcal{A}$ and is only available to $\mathcal{A}$ if the attacked instance U^k is fresh.

In order to model the forward security of the session key, we consider a game $Game^{fs-ake}$ in which the protocol is executed in the presence of the adversary $\mathcal{A}$. In this game, we provide coin tosses and oracles to $\mathcal{A}$, and then run the adversary, letting adversary $\mathcal{A}$ ask any number of queries as described above in any order. The simple restriction is that the Test oracle is available only if the queried instance U^k holds a key. The goal of the adversary is to guess the hidden bit b involved in the Test query, by outputting a guess b'. Let $Succ$ denote the event in which adversary is successful and correctly guesses the value bit b. The advantage of an adversary is defined as $Adv_{\mathcal{A}}^{fs-ake}(t,k) = 2\Pr[Succ] - 1$. The protocol is said to be forward security if $\mathcal{A}$'s advantage is negligible in the security parameter for any probability polynomial time adversary running with time t.

4 The Novel PAKE Protocol

In this section, we introduce our PAKE protocol using bilinear pairings called BP-PAKE protocol in Fig.1, and provide a rigorous proof of semantic security for it bases on the hardness of the BDH problem. Furthermore, we give the evaluation of the security and efficiency of the novel protocol.

4.1 Our PAKE Protocol

Our PAKE protocol is using bilinear pairings. Where $H_1 : \{0,1\}^* \rightarrow G_1$, $H_0, H_2 : \{0,1\}^* \rightarrow \{0,1\}^l$ are three Hash function.

$$Public\ information : Q \in G_1 = \langle P \rangle, P_s = sP, H_i$$

$$
\begin{array}{ll}
C(pw) & S(pw,s) \\
x \in_R \mathbb{Z}_q^* & \\
X = xP \quad \xrightarrow{\quad X^* = X + pwQ, C \quad} & Z_s = \hat{e}(xP, sH_1(ID_C, X)) \\
 & Auth_S = H_2(S,C,X^*,Z_S) \\
 & \\
 \xleftarrow{\quad Auth_S, S \quad} & \\
Z_C = \hat{e}(P_s, xH_1(ID_C, X)) & \\
Auth_S \stackrel{?}{=} H_2(S,C,X^*,Z_C) & \\
if\ false,\ terminates & \\
Auth_C = H_2(C,S,X^*,Z_C) & \\
SK = H_0(C,S,X^*,Z_C, pw) & \\
 \xrightarrow{\quad Auth_C \quad} & \\
 & Auth_C \stackrel{?}{=} H_2(C,S,X^*,Z_S) \\
 & if\ false,\ terminates \\
 & SK = H_0(C,S,X^*,Z_s, pw)
\end{array}
$$

Fig. 1. BP-PAKE

4.2 Security Proof

As the following theorem states, the novel PAKE protocol is secure as long as the BDH problem is hard. The security proof is in the random oracle model.

Theorem 1. Let BP-PAKE describe the password authenticated key exchange protocol associated with these primitives as defined in Fig.1. D is a uniformly distributed dictionary of size N. Let A be an adversary running within a time bound t that asks less than q_s Send queries, q_p Execute queries, and q_h hash queries. Then,

$$Adv_A^{fs-ake}(t,k) \le \frac{(q_s + q_p)^2}{q-1} + \frac{q_h^2 + 2q_s}{2^l} + \frac{2q_s}{N} + 4q_h \cdot Adv_{Abdh}^{bdh}(t,k)$$

Proof. The security proof for the proposed BP-PAKE defines a sequence of hybrid games, starting with the real attack and ending in a game in which the adversary has no advantage. Each game addresses a different security aspect. We denote S_n as the event that the adversary correctly guesses the bit b involved in the Test query. Due to the limited space, here we only present a brief sketch of the proof.

Game G_0: This is the real protocol in the random oracle model. By definition, we have $Adv_{A}^{fs-ake}(t,k) = 2\Pr[S_0] - 1$

Game G_1: In this game, we simulate the Hash oracles (H_i, i=0,1,2, but also additional Hash function $H_3, H_4 : \{0,1\}^* \rightarrow \{0,1\}^l$ which will be used later). We also simulate all the instances, as the real players would do, for the Send, Execute, Reveal and Test queries. We easily see that the game is perfectly indistinguishable from the real attack: $\Pr[S_1] = \Pr[S_0]$

Game G_2: For an easier analysis in the following, we cancel games in which some collisions *Coll* appear: collisions on the partial transcripts (C, S, X^*, $Auth_S$, $Auth_C$) and on hash values. The probability is bounded by the birthday paradox:

$$|\Pr[S_2] - \Pr[S_1]| \le \Pr[Coll] \le \frac{(q_s + q_p)^2}{2(q-1)} + \frac{q_h^2}{2^{l+1}}$$

Game G_3: In this game, we compute X^* as xP where x is random element in $\mathbb{Z}_q^*$. Meantime, we compute them as follows: $Auth_S = H_4(S,C,X^*)$, $Auth_C = H_4(C, S, X^*)$ and $SK = H_3(C,S,X^*)$, so that their values are completely independent not only from H_2 and H_0, but also from pw: $\Pr[S_3] = \frac{1}{2}$

The game G_3 and G_2 are indistinguishable unless the event *AskH* occurs: A queries the Hash functions H_0 on (C, S, X^*, $Z_{C(S)}$, pw) or H_2 on (S, C, X^*, $Z_{S(C)}$), (C, S, X^*, $Z_{S(C)}$). Thus we have $|\Pr[Succ_3] - \Pr[Succ_2]| \le \Pr[AskH]$

Game G_4: In order to evaluate the above events, we introduce BDH problem instance (U, V, W), where $U, V, W \in G_1$. We set $U=uP$, $V=sP$, $W = H_1(ID_C, U)$. A takes input tripe of (U, V, W). For a more convenient analysis, we can split the event *AskH* in 2 disjoint sub-cases:

Case1: X^* has been simulated and there is an element pw such that the tuple (S, C, X^*, $Auth_S$, $Auth_C$) is in Λ_H, with the $Auth_S$, $Auth_C$ are true. As a consequence, one can solve the BDH problem. Thus, we have $\Pr[Case1] \le q_h \cdot Adv_{Abdh}^{bdh}(t,k)$.

Case2: X^* has been produced by the adversary. Firstly, if $Auth_{S(C)}$ is the value that comes from some query of H_2, the probability is less than $\frac{1}{N} + \frac{1}{2^l}$. Secondly, adversary may distinguish the two games only when he queries oracle H_2, the probability is less than $Adv^{bdh}_{A_{bdh}}(t,k)$. Then we have $\Pr[Case2] \leq \dfrac{q_s}{N} + \dfrac{q_s}{2^l} + q_h \cdot Adv^{bdh}_{A_{bdh}}(t,k)$. As

a conclusion, $\Pr[\text{AskH}] \leq \dfrac{q_s}{N} + \dfrac{q_s}{2^l} + 2q_h \cdot Adv^{bdh}_{A_{bdh}}(t,k)$

Combining all the above equations, one gets the announced result.

4.3 Evaluation of Efficiency and Security

In this subsection, we compare the security properties and efficiency of the improved protocol with other two protocols, which is summarized in Table 2. With respect to efficiency, we denote computation cost be measured in numbers of scalar multiplications (e.g. xP), hash operations. For security properties, we consider three main aspects: identity protection (IDP), key compromise impersonation attack (EKCIA), off-line dictionary attack (OLDA) and replay attack (RA). Apparently, our protocol satisfies all security requirements and is quite efficient.

Table 2. Comparison of efficiency and security

Protocol	C-C	H-O	S-M	IDP	EKCIA	OLDA	RA
Das [3]	716	2	3	F	F	F	F
Juang [6]	1062	10	3	T	F	T	T
This paper	1068	8	3	T	T	T	T

Note: T for secure, F for insecure, C-C: communication cost (bits). H-O: the number of hash operations, S-M: the number of total scalar multiplications.

5 Conclusion

In this paper, we propose an efficient password authenticated key exchange protocol using bilinear pairings. The novel protocol can not only resist all the existing attacks, but also provide the property of the perfect forward secrecy. Furthermore, this paper also gives the rigorous security proof of the novel protocol under the Bilinear Diffie-Hellman assumption in the random oracle model. When compared with previous protocols, our protocol has stronger security and more efficiency.

References

1. Lamport, L.: Password Authentication with Insecure Communication. Communications of ACM 24, 28–30 (1981)
2. Shimizu, A., Horioka, T., Inagaki, H.: A Password Authentication Method for Contents Communication on the Internet. IEICE Transactions on Communications E81-B(8), 1666–1673 (1998)
3. Das, M.L., Saxena, A., Gulati, V.P., Phatak, D.B.: A Novel Remote User Authentication Scheme Using Bilinear Pairings. Computers & Security 25(3), 184–189 (2006)

4. Goriparthi, T., Das, M.L., Negi, A., Saxena, A.: Cryptanalysis of Recently Proposed Remote User Authentication Schemes, http://eprint.iacr.org/2006/028.pdf
5. Juang, W.S., Nien, W.K.: Efficient Password Authenticated Key Agreement Using Bilinear Pairings. Mathematical and Computer Modelling 47, 1238–1245 (2008)
6. Bellare, M., Rogaway, P.: Provably Secure Session Key Distribution: the Three PartyCase. In: STOC 1995, pp. 57–66. ACM, New York (1995)
7. Bellare, M., Pointcheval, D., Rogaway, P.: Authenticated Key Exchange Secure against Dictionary Attacks. In: Preneel, B. (ed.) EUROCRYPT 2000. LNCS, vol. 1807, pp. 139–155. Springer, Heidelberg (2000)

A New Analytical Model and Protocol for Mobile Ad-Hoc Networks Based on Time Varying Behavior of Nodes

Hamed Ranjzad, Akbar Ghaffar, and Pour Rahbar

Computer Networks Research Lab, Sahand University of Technology, Tabriz, Iran
hamedranjzad@gmail.com

Abstract. In this paper, a new model for time varying behavior of ad-hoc networks is proposed. The additions and deletions of connection links in an ad-hoc network, which arise from mobility nature of nodes, result in transient time behavior for nodes in which loads of buffers vary instantly and may damage buffers. In our protocol, the transient behavior is eliminated and the required buffer size for nodes would be predictable. We consider the brown mobility of molecules for modeling the random mobility of nodes. We have presented numerical results for time behavior of our mobility model.

Keywords: ad-hoc networks, time varying behavior, transient time, brown mobility model.

1 Introduction

Wireless communication between mobile users is becoming more popular than ever before. This is due to the technological advances in laptop computers and wireless communication devices such as wireless modems and wireless LANs. This technology has lead to lower prices and higher data rates. Nowadays, mobile ad-hoc networks are widely used in communication environments. Since these networks do not require any fixed infrastructure, they can be established quickly. This is useful for applications such as disaster recovery situations, where a rapid deployment of a communication network is needed. Many protocols have been proposed for routing of ad-hoc networks. Mainly, these protocols are based on minimizing the number of hops, e.g. DSR, CBR, AODV, CBRP, and DSDV [1, 2, 3, 4]. However, there is little work on studying the dynamic behavior of ad-hoc networks.

In [5], node queuing model based on Point wise Stationary Fluid Flow Approximation (PSFFA) has been investigated. Differential equation model of an M/M/1 queue from the Chapman-Kolmogorov is given in [6]. The steady-state Simulation of Queuing Processes is described in [7]. In [8], the behavior of ad-hoc networks has been investigated and a queuing model, based on fluid flow, has been proposed for time behavior of ad-hoc networks, called Discrete Time Behavior Model (DTBM). DTBM results in transient state in which the load of buffers face a huge variance when a link is disconnected (see [8]). This is called damaging the buffers of nodes in this paper. In DTBM, the size of buffers should be greater than the real size that is required in steady state, so that, this model yields in damaging of buffers and

J.H. Park et al. (Eds.): ISA 2009, CCIS 36, pp. 57–67, 2009.
© Springer-Verlag Berlin Heidelberg 2009

wasting their usage. In all the models described in [5, 6, 7, 8], the status of link connection between any two nodes is discrete value, i.e. either 0 or 1. These models can only represent the connection and disconnection between any two nodes.

Our objective in this paper is to develop a new model called Adaptive Time Behavior Model (ATBM) that results in a new adaptive protocol called Adaptive Time Behavior Protocol (ATBP). This new protocol prevents from transient behaviors and can improve the throughput of ad-hoc networks. In addition to represent connection and disconnection between nodes, our new model can represent the reinforcement and attenuation of the links between any two nodes.

The organization of this paper is as follows. In Section 2, mobility model of ad-hoc nodes is proposed. Section 3 discusses the time behavior model of ad-hoc network's nodes. Section 4 describes mobility models for ad-hoc network's nodes. In Section 5, we present numerical results for time behavior of nodes. Section 6 concludes the paper.

2 Mobility Modeling of Ad-Hoc Nodes

Consider an ad-hoc network with M nodes, where the connections of these nodes can be demonstrated with a $M \times M$ matrix. This matrix is called adjustment matrix in which the connection between two nodes i and j at time t is determined with $a_{ij}(t)$, $a_{ji}(t)$ (see matrix $A(t)$ below).

$$A(t) = \begin{bmatrix} a_{11}(t) & a_{12}(t) & \cdots & a_{1M}(t) \\ a_{21}(t) & a_{22}(t) & \cdots & a_{2M}(t) \\ \vdots & \vdots & \vdots & \vdots \\ a_{M1}(t) & a_{M2}(t) & \cdots & a_{MM}(t) \end{bmatrix}$$

Since the connectivity between two nodes depends on the radio power between them, which follows from antenna pattern and distance of two nodes, we can describe the entries of an adjustment matrix as power loss between two nodes. Loss L between two nodes i and j at time t is determined by Eq.(1) as

$$Li, j = (\frac{4\pi \ d_{i,j}(t)}{\lambda})^2 \tag{1}$$

where $d_{ij}(t)$ is the distance between node i and j and λ is the wavelength of transmitted beam. Therefore, we should associate $a_{ij}(t)$ with $d_{ij}(t)$. For this purpose, we can use Eq.(2) in which $a_{ij}(t)$ has a value between 0 and 1.

$$a_{i,j}(t)\alpha \frac{1}{1+\sqrt[3]{d_{i,j}(t)}}$$

$$a_{i,j}(t) = \frac{k}{1+\sqrt[3]{d_{i,j}(t)}} \tag{2}$$

where, K is a factor that depends on the environmental conditions such as physical obstacles. This equation obviously associates the link of two nodes to the distance between them. If the distance between two nodes is greater than a threshold value, the received power by nodes will be smaller than the sensitivity power of antennas, and therefore, the link of two nodes will fail. Hence, $a_{ij}(t)$ can be determined by

$$a_{i,j}(t) = \begin{cases} \dfrac{1}{1+\sqrt[3]{di,j(t)}} & if\ d_{i,j}(t) < d_{threshold}\ i,j \\ 0 & otherwise \end{cases} \tag{3}$$

- By defining $P_R\ i,j(t)$ as the received power by node j from node i; the parameters G_T and G_R as the transmitter and receiver antennas gain respectively; and the parameter G as the total gain of the receiver and transmitter antenna which is defined as $G=G_TG_R$, we have the following equation obtained from [15]

$$P_R i, j(t) = \frac{P_T G \lambda^2}{(4\pi d_{i,j}(t))^2} = \frac{P_T G_T G_R \lambda^2}{(4\pi d_{i,j}(t))^2} \tag{4}$$

where P_T is the output power of the transmitter antenna. Here, we have $G_T = \frac{4\pi A_T}{\lambda^2}$ and $G_R = \frac{4\pi A_R}{\lambda^2}$, where A_T and A_R are the effective area of the transmitter and receiver antennas respectively. When the distance between two nodes reaches to threshold, Eq.(4) is changed to Eq.(5) as

$$P_{threshold} i, j = \frac{P_{T \max} G_T G_R \lambda^2}{(4\pi d_{threshold} i, j)^2} = \frac{P_{T \max} A_T A_R}{(\lambda d_{threshold} i, j)^2} \tag{5}$$

where P_{TMAX} is the maximum output power of the transmitter antenna when the distance between two nodes reaches to threshold value, and is a priori-known value for each antenna. Here, $P_{threshold}\ i,j$ is the threshold power between nodes i and j, $P_{sensitivity}\ i,j$ is the sensitivity power between nodes i and j which is defined as a property for antennas and equals $P_{sensivity} i, j = P_{threshold} i, j$.

Now, the threshold for distance can be calculated using Eq. (5) as:

$$d_{threshold} i, j = \frac{1}{\lambda} \sqrt{\frac{P_{T \max} A_T A_R}{P_{sensivity} i, j}} \tag{6}$$

Clearly, by moving nodes, the topology of an ad-hoc network and the entries of the adjustment matrix can vary. If all nodes have identical receiver and transmitter antennas, $d_{threshold}$ will be equal for all node pairs. Otherwise, $d_{threshold}$ will depend on any nodes pair.

3   Time Behavior Modeling of Nodes

In order to model the time behavior of ad-hoc network nodes, we have developed multi-traffic class M/M/1 fluid flow model explained in [8]. A node can be described by a set of S nonlinear differential equations of the form Eq.(7), which represents the time varying behavior of each traffic class separately. The class of each traffic is determined by final destination of that class. In this equation, the parameter $x_l(t)$

represents the average number of packets of class l in the queuing system at time t, and C is the wireless link capacity. There are S different classes of packets arriving at the node with the average arrival rates $\lambda_1(t)$, $\lambda_2(t)$, .., $\lambda_S(t)$. The length of packets is distributed exponentially with mean $1/\mu$. The system equations can be solved using the numerical integration approach.

$$x^{\bullet}{}_1(t) = -\mu C \left(\frac{x_1(t)}{1 + \sum_{j=1}^{S} x_j(t)} \right) + \lambda_1(t) \quad \forall l = 1,2,...S \tag{7}$$

3.1 Adaptive Time Behavior Model (ATBM)

We have improved DTBM described in [8] by using continuous values for $a_{ij}(t)$. Note that in [8], $a_{ij}(t)$ is equal to either 0 or 1 which describes the disconnection and connection between nodes i and j respectively. By considering continuous values for $a_{ij}(t)$, traffic rate between two nodes will depend on the distance between them.

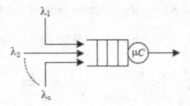

Fig. 1. The model of a node with S classes of traffic

The Eq.(10) of [8] determines an ad-hoc network fluid-flow. In that model, $r_{ik}{}^{j}(t)$ is defined as a routing variable from node i to node k for traffic destined to node j. The value of the routing variable at any point in time depends on the specific routing scheme used in the network. We have eliminated this variable in the ATBM model because in ATBM traffic rate has been adapted with distances among nodes, and $r_{ik}{}^{j}(t)$ has been inserted in $a_{ik}(t)$. Therefore, no knowledge about the routing protocol is required. The flow out of node i of class j traffic into node k and the flow of class j traffic into node i from node l are given by Eq.(8) and Eq.(9) respectively.

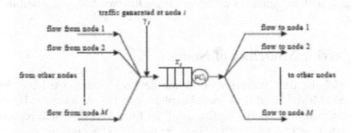

Fig. 2. The queuing model of an arbitrary node i

$$\mu C_i \left(\frac{x_i^{\,j}(t)}{1 + \sum\limits_{\substack{l=1 \\ l \neq i}}^{M} x_i^{\,l}(t)} \right) (a_{ik}(t)) \tag{8}$$

$$\mu C_l \left(\frac{x_l^{\,j}(t)}{1 + \sum\limits_{\substack{k=1 \\ k \neq l}}^{M} x_l^{\,k}(t)} \right) (a_{lj}(t)) \tag{9}$$

Corresponding ad-hoc network fluid-flow model is determined by summing the flows in and flows out over all possible nodes (see Eq.(10)).

$$\dot{x}_i^{\,j}(t) = -\mu C_i \left(\frac{x_i^{\,j}(t)}{1 + \sum\limits_{\substack{l=1 \\ l \neq i}}^{M} x_i^{\,l}(t)} \right) \sum\limits_{\substack{k=1 \\ k \neq i}}^{M} a_{ik}(t) + \gamma_i^{\,j}(t) + \sum\limits_{\substack{l=1 \\ l \neq j}}^{M} \mu C_l \left(\frac{x_l^{\,j}(t)}{1 + \sum\limits_{\substack{k=1 \\ k \neq l}}^{M} x_l^{\,k}(t)} \right) (a_{li}(t)) \tag{10}$$

where $\gamma_i^{\,j}$ is the rate of flow of class j traffic generated in node i into the same node queue.

ATBM is a protocol in which the traffic rate is adapted with the distance between nodes, where we have named this protocol ATBP. In transient-state under ATBP, the size of buffers would be predictable with the traffic load of network. However, in transient-state under DTBM, since the computed buffer size is not usable the size of buffers should be chosen bigger than the required size for steady state. This clearly wastes buffers in the previous model.

By increasing the distance between nodes, delay time and error probability also increase. In this state, our protocol decreases data rate. If the distance between nodes are decreased, delay time and error probability are reduced, where in this state ATBP increases data rate. Hence, it is expected that the throughput of network to increase. The other advantage of ATBM is its independence of time behavior of nodes from the speed of topology variances which arise from the intelligence of nodes and adaptive data rate of ATBP. This independence is shown in Section 5. However, in the DTBM, the behavior of nodes depends on the speed of topology changes because data rate between any two nodes is independent of the distance between them.

4 Mobility Model for Ad-Hoc Nodes

In order to simulate the time behavior of ad-hoc network nodes, we have used a random mechanic model. This model is based on the brown mobility of molecules. This mobility is defined as follows:

Random Walk Mobility Model (RWMM): A simple mobility model based on random directions and speeds. The RWMM was first described mathematically by Einstein in 1926. Since many entities in nature move in extremely unpredictable

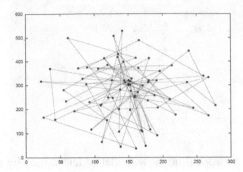

Fig. 3. Traveling pattern of a mobile node using the 2-D RWMM (time)

ways, the RWMM was developed to mimic this erratic movement. In this mobility model, a mobile node moves from its current location to a new location by randomly choosing a direction and speed in which to travel. The new speed and direction are both chosen from pre-defined ranges, [speed min, speed max] and $[0, 2\pi]$ respectively. Each movement in the RWMM occurs in either a constant time interval t or a constant distance traveled d, at the end of which a new direction and speed are calculated. If a mobile node which moves according to this model reaches a simulation boundary, it "bounces" off the simulation border with an angle determined by the incoming direction. Fig.3 shows an example of the movement observed from this model. Many derivatives of the RWMM have been developed including the 1-D, 2-D, 3-D, and d-D walks. In 1921, Polya proved that a random walk on a one or two-dimensional surface returns to the origin with complete certainty, i.e., a probability of 1.0. This characteristic ensures that the random walk represents a mobility model that tests the movements of entities around their starting points, without worrying about the entities that wander away from and never to return [9, 10, 11, 12, 13, 14].

5 Numerical Results for Time Behavior of Nodes

Here, we present the numerical results for time behavior of nodes based on our new model and protocol and compare them with the model that has been presented in [8]. We have presented numerical results for the network with three nodes in Fig.4 and Fig.5. We set $c_1=c_2=c_3=20$ and $\mu=0.5$ which corresponds to a normalized server capacity of one packet per second. For the numerical solution of the differential equations, the fifth order Runge-Kutta routine provided in MATLAB has been utilized. To solve a differential equation, the Runge-Kutta routine requires a time step Δt parameter. Here, various values are assigned to time step Δt (decreasing from 1.0 to 0.1), where over each time step, an equation is solved. This procedure is repeated until decreasing the time step Δt results in no change in the numerical values. We have assumed that the effective area of any transmitter and receiver antennas is 25cm^2, P_{Tmax} is 0dbm and $P_{sensitivity}$ is equal to -80dbm, frequency of transmitted beam is 5GHz. Then, according to Eq.(6), threshold distances will be approximately 400 meters. For simplicity in the numerical solution, we have assumed that all nodes are

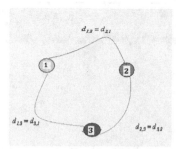

Fig. 4. A mobility and connectivity scenario

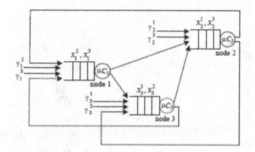

Fig. 5. The queuing model of a 3-node ad-hoc network

identical, and therefore, the threshold distance value $d_{threshold}$ is always 400meters for all paired nodes which corresponds to 0.11 in $a_{i,j}$ value according to Eq.(3). maximum value of $a_{i,j}$ which is 1.0 in our model.

We have done our simulations in three cases as follows:

Case 1: First we have assumed load to be $\gamma_{12}(t)=0.18$, $\gamma_{13}(t)=0.22$, $\gamma_{21}(t)=018$, $\gamma_{23}(t)=0.22$, $\gamma_{31}(t)=0.18$, and $\gamma_{32}(t)=0.22$. Topology of nodes varies based on RWMM. As shown in Fig.6, load of buffers oscillates approximately around a fixed value which only depends on load condition. A rising section is due to the decrease of distance between two nodes. On the other hand, a falling section is because of the increase of the distances between two nodes. There are no transient states in buffers and the required buffer size can be predictable based on load conditions.

Case 2: In order to investigate the traffic load effect on the time behavior of nodes, we have increased traffic loads to $\gamma_{12}(t)=0.25$, $\gamma_{13}(t)=0.35$, $\gamma_{21}(t)=0.35$, $\gamma_{23}(t)=0.25$, $\gamma_{31}(t)=0.30$, and $\gamma_{32}(t)=0.30$. Mobility conditions and topology are as the same as the previous considerations. Simulation results for load increasing effect are shown in Fig.7. Comparing Fig.7 with Fig.6, we can say that the load of buffers has increased because of the increase of traffic load. There is no transient state in this case as well.

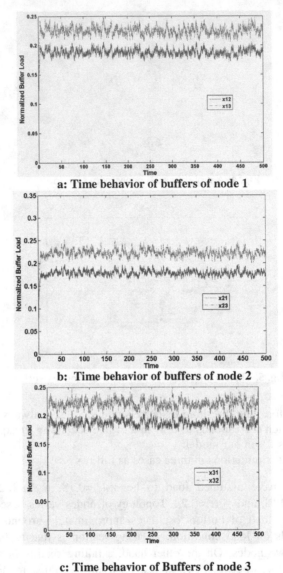

a: Time behavior of buffers of node 1

b: Time behavior of buffers of node 2

c: Time behavior of Buffers of node 3

Fig. 6. Network buffers load in Case 1

Case 3: We have investigated the effect of the speed of topology variance on the time behavior of nodes by increasing the variance of speed. We have found that in the ATBM model (see Fig. 8), the load of nodes buffers is independent of topology variances speed in steady state. Here, traffic loads are the same as the traffic load in Case 1. In the DTBM model, the rapid variance of network topology increases buffer load in steady state which is an undesirable issue in network. The values which load of buffer oscillates around them are the same in Fig.6 and Fig.8. But, the number of oscillations has increased in Fig.8 because of increasing the speed of topology variance.

Comparing the results obtained based on DTBM (see [8]) shows that ATBM is more suitable than DTBM in terms of eliminating the transient conditions in buffers, i.e., there is no huge variation in the number of packets arriving at the buffers of nodes.

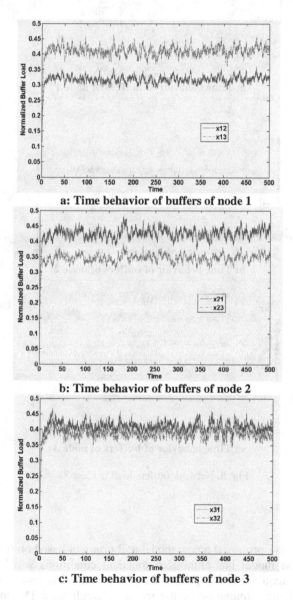

a: Time behavior of buffers of node 1

b: Time behavior of buffers of node 2

c: Time behavior of buffers of node 3

Fig. 7. Network buffers load in Case 2

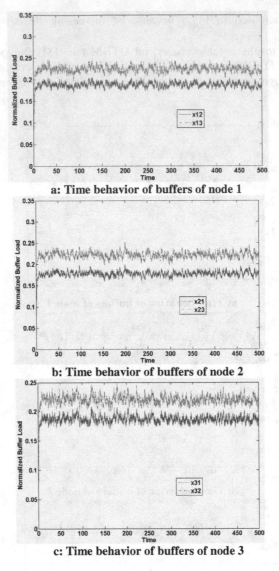

a: Time behavior of buffers of node 1

b: Time behavior of buffers of node 2

c: Time behavior of buffers of node 3

Fig. 8. Network buffers load in Case 3

6 Conclusion

In this paper, we have proposed a new model and protocol based on time behavior of
nodes. Our ATBM model has eliminated transient conditions which may damage
buffers of nodes. Required buffer size in the ATBM model is less than the previous
model because of the elimination of the transient conditions. The model we have
provided not only represents connection and disconnection between nodes, but also
represents the reinforcement and attenuation of the links between any two nodes.

Adaptive protocol resulting from this model can also improve throughput of network. We will investigate throughput improvements in our future work.

Acknowledgement

This research is supported by Iran Telecommunication Research Center, Ministry of Communication and Information Technology of Iran.

References

[1] Qin, L., Kunz, T.: Survey on Mobile Ad-Hoc Network Routing Protocols and Cross-Layer Design, Systems and Computer Engineering, Technical Report SCE-04-14 (August 2004)

[2] Royer, E.M., Toh, C.K.: A Review of Current Routing Protocols for Ad-Hoc Mobile Wireless Networks. IEEE Personal Communications (April 1999)

[3] Perkins, C.E., Royer, E.M., Das, S., Marina, M.: Performance Comparison of Two On-demand Routing Protocols for Ad Hoc Networks. IEEE Personal Communications (February 2001)

[4] Perkins, C.E., Royer, E.M., Das, S.R.: Ad-hoc On demand Distance Vector (AODV) Routing. IETF Internet Draft (January 2002)

[5] Wang, W., Tipper, D., Banerjee, S.: A Simple Approximation for Modeling non Stationary Queues. In: Proc. IEEE INFOCOM 1996, San Francisco, CA (1996)

[6] Rider, K.: A Simple Approximation to the Average Queue Size in the Time Dependent M/M/1 queue. Journal of ACM 23(2), 361–367 (1976)

[7] Pawlikowski, K.: Steady-State Simulation of Queuing Processes: A Survey of Problems and Solutions. ACM Computing Surveys 22(2), 123–170 (1990)

[8] Tipper, D., Qian, Y., Hou, X.: Modeling the Time Varying Behavior of Mobile Ad-Hoc. In: Proc. the 7th ACM International Symposium on Modeling, Analysis and Simulation of Wireless and Mobile Systems, Venezia, Italy (October 2004)

[9] Saha, A.K., Johnson, D.B.: Modeling Mobility for Vehicular Ad Hoc Networks. In: Proc. the 1st ACM International Workshop on Vehicular Ad Hoc Networks, pp. 91–92 (2004)

[10] Lin, G., Noubir, G., Rajaraman, R.: Mobility Models for Ad hoc Network Simulation. In: IEEE INFOCOM 2004 (2004)

[11] Jardosh, A., Royer, E.M.B., Almeroth, K.C., Suri, S.: Towards Realistic Mobility Models for Mobile Ad hoc Networks. In: MobiCom 2003, San Diego, California, USA (September 2003)

[12] Bhattacharjee, D., Rao, A., Shah, C., Shah, M.: Faculty: Ahmed Helmy, Empirical Modeling of Campus-wide Pedestrian Mobility: Observations on the USC Campus. In: IEEE 60th Vehicular Technology Conference, September 2004, pp. 2887–2891 (2004)

[13] Zonoozi, M., Dassanayake, P.: User mobility modeling and characterization of mobility pattern. IEEE Journal on Selected Areas in Communications 15(7), 1239–1252 (1997)

[14] Weisstein, E.W.: The CRC Concise Encyclopedia of Mathematics. CRC Press, Boca Raton (1998)

Context-Based E-Health System Access Control Mechanism

Fahed Al-Neyadi and Jemal H. Abawajy

Deakin University,
Pervasive Computing and Network Research Group,
School of Engineering and Information Technology,
Melbourne, Vic. Australia
{fmal,jemal}@deakin.edu.au

Abstract. E-Health systems logically demand a sufficiently fine-grained authorization policy for access control. The access to medical information should not be just role-based but should also include the contextual condition of the role to access data. In this paper, we present a mechanism to extend the standard role-based access control to incorporate contextual information for making access control decisions in e-health application. We present an architecture consisting of authorisation and context infrastructure that work cooperatively to grant access rights based on context-aware authorization policies and context information.

Keywords: access control, autherisation, security, e-health, context-aware.

1 Introduction

Healthcare delivery is a highly complex process and an increasingly collaborative enterprise involving a broad range of healthcare services provided by many individuals and organizations [5]. The rapid global deployment of the Internet and Web is the enabler of a new generation of e-healthcare applications. Standards such as the Health Level Seven (HL7) specifications facilitate dissimilar healthcare applications to exchange key sets of clinical and administrative data [13]. These technological developments will enable future large-scale healthcare systems to engage many diverse healthcare enterprises collaborating in patient care, including doctors, private physicians, private clinics, hospitals, dentists, pharmacies, drug and insurance companies [14]. As the interconnection between medical systems becomes more prevalent and the deployment becomes extensive, the security violations are bound to increase [12].

In this paper, we address the problem of access control of the e-health system resources and information. Access control is a key security component which guarantees that a service can only be accessed by users who have the rights and the privileges to use that service. The provision of a security architecture that can ensure the privacy and security of sensitive healthcare data is still an open question [6]. Today, security administration is costly and prone to error because administrators usually specify access control lists for

J.H. Park et al. (Eds.): ISA 2009, CCIS 36, pp. 68–77, 2009.
© Springer-Verlag Berlin Heidelberg 2009

each user on the system individually. Healthcare systems have complicated access rules for the reason that they have many roles in the system and their interconnecting access privileges. Traditional access control mechanisms such as access control list break down in such an environments and a fine-grained access control mechanism that changes the privilege of a user dynamically based on context information is required. Context-based access control is a solution to impose authorization rules for access control in e-health systems so that the healthcare professionals can get access to patient data on demand and in emergency situations without compromising with the security, privacy and confidentiality of patient data.

In this paper, we propose a context-based access control mechanism which guarantees that e-Health services can only be accessed by users who have the rights and the privileges to use that e-Health service. The proposed context-based access control mechanism is an extension of the X-GTRBAC framework [1] to offer a context-based access control model for e-health Web Services. The proposed approach is able to provide authorisation rules to enforce access control not only on the basis of information of the roles but it also incorporates the contextual information; and it can be implemented via Web Services.

The rest of the paper is organised as follows. In Section 2, we review the related work. In Section 3, we describe the proposed work that extends the X-GTRBAC to incorporate contextual information for making access control decisions in the e-health system. The conclusions and future directions are discussed in Section 4.

2 Related Work

Health care domain requires appropriate measures at all times to guard health care medical information and functionality. The ambiguity of how patient data can be secured which exist in incongruent systems, fear of identity theft, abiding by the legislation which regulates the healthcare industry, these are all the matters that healthcare providers should be obliged to guarantee uninterrupted functioning and secure, quick to respond patient care. The suitability of the actions taken to safeguard the medical information keeps on changing with the advancement and availability of new technologies and with the changes in the legislations which regulate e-health services.

Access control is a key security component which guarantees that a service can only be accessed by users who have the rights and the privileges to use that service. Protecting patients' private information is one of the most demanding concerns in the design and implementation of modern e-Health systems. Moreover, healthcare systems have complicated access rules for the reason that they have many roles in the system and their interconnecting access privileges. Sensible healthcare IT systems have got to hold up thousands of users, roles, objects, and permissions. Our goal is to sustain evolvable access control so that its enforcement can be configured and modified to include variations.

E-Health systems logically demand a sufficiently fine-grained authorization policy for access control. Role-based access control (RBAC) [4] is a widely used access control method in healthcare systems. RBAC can be implemented to define a diverse set of access control policies and it also simplifies authorization administration in large enterprises. RBAC assures a lesser amount of composite management than the conventional way, where users are managed as individuals or in groups and assigned roles. It also offers an improved outline of the privileges that must be withdrawn, therefore enhancing the safety measures of the systems. But it cannot provide the complex and fine-grained authorization policies that the healthcare systems desire.

A temporal RBAC (TRBAC) [10] model has also been proposed to handle such scenarios where the users may be restricted to assume roles at predefined time periods, and the roles may be invoked on pre-specified intervals of time depending upon when certain actions are permitted. A Generalized Temporal Role-Based Access Control (GTRBAC) model [2] extends the syntactic structure of the TRBAC model, which allows expressing periodic and duration constraints on roles, user-role assignments, and role-permission assignments, as well as several activation constraints including cardinality constraints and maximum active duration constraints.

The X-GTRBAC framework [1] augments the GTRBAC model with XML to allow for supporting the policy enforcement in a distributed heterogeneous environment. An XML schema provides more expressive power and support for data types as well as use of credentials which are essential when dealing with heterogeneity. However, the standard RBAC and its variants are not able to reflect various dynamic elements of the current health care environment. Unfortunately, the current solutions which are built on RBAC models are static and capable of merely imposing temporal constraints on roles. They cannot enforce authorization rules that are based on contextual information and thus do not deal with the complex security demands of the healthcare systems. Present e-health systems need an infrastructure which can enforce authorization policies based on the current situation of the user.

The access to medical information should not be just role-based but should also include the contextual condition of the role to access data. To this end, we presented a context-based access control model for e-health Web Services. The mechanism extends the X-GTRBAC to incorporate contextual constraints for making access control decisions in e-health systems.

3   Context-Aware Access Control Model

Future large-scale healthcare systems will engage many diverse businesses collaborating in patient care, including doctors, private physicians, private clinics, hospitals, dentists, pharmacies, drug and insurance companies. A context-based access control technique offers the security given by both the user-based and role-based access control and takes it one step further by including the context for making access control decisions. Context-based access control takes into account the person attempting to access the data, the type of data being accessed and the context of the transaction in which the access attempt is made. In this section, we present a framework for context-aware authorisation for e-Health environments. We present an architecture consisting of authorization infrastructure and context infrastructure.

3.1   Contextual Model

We adapt the terminologies of [9] to describe the context model presented in this paper. We assume a finite set of data objects D, that require protection in the domain of a healthcare provider.

$$D = \{d_1, d_2, ..., d_n\}$$

Examples of the data objects maintained by the system resources include a prescription, a clinical note, a radiological report, a laboratory test result, a diagnostic image, etc. There is a set of users, U, in the system that will access the data objects in the data set of an application.

$$U = \{u_1, u_2, ..., u_n\}$$

A user is an entity (a person who uses the system or an application program in the system) whose access is being controlled. Examples of users are doctors, nurses, administrative staff, etc. At any given time, each user is associated with a set of attributes, C, that represents the set of context information such as location, health care unit, date/time, etc.

$$C = \{c_1, c_{p2}, ..., c_n\}$$

Every application has its own context set based on the context type. An application designer decides which context types will be used to denote access by analysing the security requirements. Also, the system administrators can add new ones dynamically when required.

The system also maintains a set of roles, R, and a set of permissions, P, that govern access to the system. Roles are used to grant users access to specific resources. The set of the roles that describe a set of functional responsibilities within the healthcare organization are defined as follows:

$$R = \{r_1, r_2, ..., r_n\}$$

A user (e.g., a doctor) is assigned a subset of roles from the entire role set during a session. Example of the roles include, "attending physician", "attending nurse". The potential role of a doctor can include prescribing medications, recommending treatments, and interpreting the results of an imaging test. The role of a nurse can include providing care for patients, measuring vital signs, and monitoring drug administration. The role of a medical assistant may include taking health histories, and performing laboratory tests. Roles have role activation, role revocation, and role hierarchies. A request in traditional RBAC comes from a certain user who has a set of roles associated with her. This association is achieved via that define what roles U is allowed to take on based on the responsibilities and functions of U and that the set of roles are transferred to U and can subsequently be used during access requests. This is called role activation in RBAC. Roles can be hierarchical, mutually exclusive, collaborative, or overlapping. For example, in a hospital some roles are hierarchical. The doctor role may include all privileges granted to the nurse role, which in turn includes all privileges granted to the medical assistant role. Role hierarchies are a natural generalization of organizing roles for granting responsibilities and privileges within an organization.

Each user is assigned one or more roles, and each role is assigned one or more privilege. Thus, every role that has privilege to access the resource is assigned a subset of permissions from the entire permission set, P, maintained by the system:

$$P = \{p_1, r_{p2}, ..., p_n\}$$

A role $r_m \in R$ can perform an operation $o_i \in O$ on an object $d_j \in D$,, if there is a permission $p_k \in P$ that authorises the role to perform the operation on the object. Permission is an approval to perform an operation O, on one or more protected e-health data objects:

$$O = \{o_1, o_{p2}, ..., o_n\}$$

Examples of the legal operations include reading, writing, deleting, inserting and so forth.

3.2 Conceptual Framework

Fig. 1 shows the context-based access control method architecture for the e-health system. Service request is specified in the form of $\langle u_i, d_k, o, AL \rangle$, where AL is the authentication trust level of user $u_i \in U$ that is allowed to access or manipulate an object $d_k \in D$ through an operation $o \in O$ such as read, write or execute.

In the proposed scheme, the authentication tokens are issued to the users by the authentication module and thus create an authentication trust level for that token. Based on the Service Access Request, the system decides the appropriate access policy for the demanded service. A set of constraints on the role and service name will be the foundation for this policy, and evaluated in combination with the on hand contextual information to implement fine grained access control. An access policy comprises of a compilation of access conditions.

The job of the authorization module is to monitor all service requests from the users and evaluate the information provided by the user to access the service that he/she wants. The authorization module evaluates a request based on the authorization rules and the contextual information provided by the user for a particular service. If the information satisfies the prerequisites of a service then the user is granted permission for that service. The Document composition module (DCM) compiles the policy documents and contains the XML-policy base which has the policy information. The XML-Policy sheets have the information which is used to implement the authorization constraints. The XML-policies of an enterprise are permitted by the GTRBAC framework to be specified and imposed through a Java-based GUI-enabled application whose code is already integrated in a Web browser by a mechanism provided by Java. More explicitly, the users are granted or denied permission depending on the roles which they are assigned to as per the XURAS (XML User-to-Role Assignment Sheet) policy sheet and the related permissions per the XPRAS (XML Permission-to-Role Assignment Sheet). The XML-Parser and the

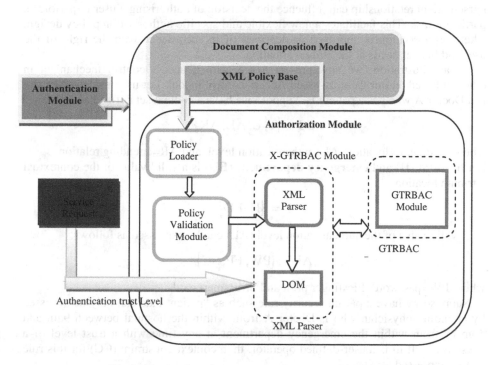

Fig. 1. Context-based access control system architecture

GTRBAC processor are the two main parts of the system. The XML parser forwards the DOM instance of the parsed XML documents to the GTRBAC processor. The GTRBAC processor has the GTRBAC module which controls and implements the policy according to the policy sheets supplied by the XML policy base [1].

We now give an example to show how the system works. Consider that a pathologist has the right to read and write the pathology reports of a patient, but if he/she only asks to read the patient pathology report then the pathologist is only given a read permission. A pathologist can log on to the system with any identification technology available on his system. An authentication token including the user details and the authentication trust level of identification technology is send to the Authorization module of the system. If the pathologist uses a username and password to log on to the system then he is given a permission only to read, if there exists a policy specification that "a pathologist should need an authentication level of a password to read data and an authentication trust level of a fingerprint to write data". To write data the pathologist will again have to log on to the system using a fingerprint as the identification technology.

3.3   Authorization Framework

Contextual authorizations can be included into the existing RBAC models which will increase the expressive power to classify access control policies. At the time of access request the contextual information which is provided by the user, such as nurse/patient relationship can influence the decision of authorising a user to perform a particular task. This facilitates a new flexible and specific authorisation policy design, where authorisation is approved or deprived of in accordance with the right of the user and his/her needs at the current situation.

As an illustration, we now present a scenario of access control mechanism in e-health based on our Context-based Access control model. Let us consider that there is a Doctor A who has a patient B. Suppose we have a context set defined as follows:

$$CS = \{T, L, AL, AR\}$$

where T=time, L=location, AL=authentication level, and AR=attending relation.
Let **hospital (H)** and **emergency department (ED)** is a valid value of the contextual attribute location:

$$L = \{H, ED\}$$

A valid value of the authentication level (AL) can be expressed as follows:

$$AL = \{PW, FP, SC\}$$

where PW=password, FP=finger print and SM=smart card.

Suppose we have a partial security rule such as "patient data can only be accessed by attending physician who is Doctor A from within the hospital between 9am and 4pm or from within the emergency department at any time with a trust level of a "password". If **in** is a user-defined operator, then context constraint (CC) for this rule can be expressed as:

$$CC = (AR = A \cap 9:00 \leq T \leq 16:00 \cap L = "H" \cap AL \geq "PW") \cup$$
$$(AR = A \cap L = "ED" \cap AL \geq "PW")$$

This is a simple scenario where the patient B and the Doctor A has an attending relation. But if Doctor A is not present in the hospital and patient B is in the emergency department and needs immediate medical attention, then the present doctor in the emergency department will need to view the medical records of the patient to check for any allergies, blood pressure etc before starting the treatment.

To solve such complex scenarios the system administrators can add one more clause with the existing context constraint such as "patient data can only be accessed by attending physician who is Doctor A from within the hospital between 9am and 4pm or from within the emergency department at any time with a trust level of a password; otherwise a higher level of trust such as a finger print of the doctor present at the emergency department is required to view the patient records". If "in" is a user-defined operator and "emergency department" is a valid value of the contextual attribute space, then this rule can be expressed as follows:

$$CC = (AR = A \cap 9:00 \leq T \leq 16:00 \cap L = "H" \cap AL \geq "P") \cup$$
$$(AR = A \cap L = "ED" \cap l \geq "PW") \cup$$
$$(AR = Doctor \cap L = "ED" \cap AL = "FP")$$

The values of the supplied runtime context parameters are compared with context constraint attributes for the requested service and based on this the system will give an authorization decision. In both the conditions given above the contextual information satisfies the access conditions for the given service.

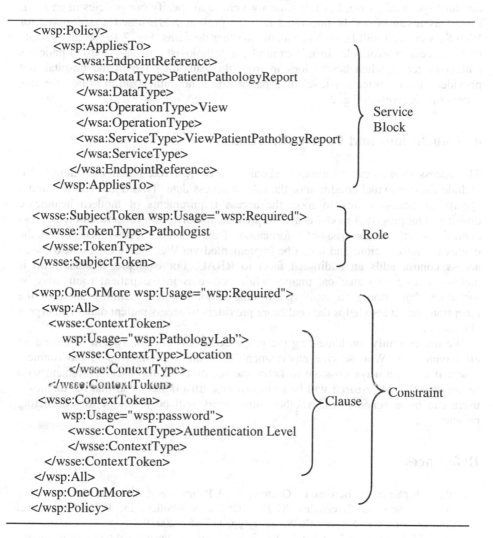

```
<wsp:Policy>
    <wsp:AppliesTo>
        <wsa:EndpointReference>
        <wsa:DataType>PatientPathologyReport
        </wsa:DataType>
        <wsa:OperationType>View
        </wsa:OperationType>
        <wsa:ServiceType>ViewPatientPathologyReport
        </wsa:ServiceType>
        </wsa:EndpointReference>
    </wsp:AppliesTo>

<wsse:SubjectToken wsp:Usage="wsp:Required">
  <wsse:TokenType>Pathologist
  </wsse:TokenType>
</wsse:SubjectToken>

<wsp:OneOrMore wsp:Usage="wsp:Required">
  <wsp:All>
    <wsse:ContextToken>
      wsp:Usage="wsp:PathologyLab">
      <wsse:ContextType>Location
      </wsse:ContextType>
    </wsse:ContextToken>
    <wsse:ContextToken>
      wsp:Usage="wsp:password">
      <wsse:ContextType>Authentication Level
      </wsse:ContextType>
    </wsse:ContextToken>
  </wsp:All>
</wsp:OneOrMore>
</wsp:Policy>
```

Service Block

Role

Clause

Constraint

Fig. 2. Policy specification for access to services

3.4 Policy Specification for Access to Services

An access policy specification in our context-based access control framework indicates which role can access which types of services under some context conditions. In e-health systems, it is not only a hospital that access medical information but there are other participants as well such as insurance companies, pharmacies, private clinics who access patient information to do their business.

Although the authorization engine uses the access policies for access control decisions but this policy specifications is also needed to be exchanged to other domains specified above. For this reason we chose to specify our policies in an XML format as it can be easily integrated into the present XML-based architectures for Web Services and will be understandable to other domains. Fig. 2 shows an example of the access control rule. In this example, a pathologist can only view a patient's pathology report when he/she logs in from the pathology lab in the hospital and provides an authentication level of a password." The authorization policy for this access rule is given in Fig. 2.

4 Conclusions and Future Directions

The access to medical information should not be just role-based but should also include the contextual condition of the role to access data. Traditional RBAC cannot specify an access policy to meet the access requirements of modern healthcare domains. Our proposed model is able to provide authorization rules to enforce access control not only on the basis of information of the roles but it also incorporates the contextual information; and it can be implemented via Web Services. Context-based access control adds an additional facet to RBAC. For example, a nurse who is authorized to access medical images while he/she is in the patient room may be forbidden from doing so while performing reimbursement administration in the reception area. It also helps the healthcare providers to access patient data in an urgent situation.

We are currently implementing the proposed access control system to ensure its effectiveness in Web service environment. E-health is a distributed environment where it is not always possible to know the identities of the user beforehand so a future direction of research will be to incorporate trust domains so that the unknown users can be assigned roles. Another future work will be to check for conflicting policies.

References

1. Bhatti, R., Sanz, D., Bertino, E., Ghafoor, A.: A Policy-Based Authorization Framework for Web Services: Integrating XGTRBAC and WS-Policy. In: IEEE International Conference on Web Services (ICWS 2007), pp. 447–454 (2007)
2. Joshi, J.B.D., Bertino, E., Elisa, L., Ghafoor, A., Arif: A generalized temporal role-based access control model. IEEE Transactions on Knowledge and Data 17(1), 4–23 (2005)
3. Eysenbach, G.: What is e-health? Journal of Medical Internet Research 1 3(2), e20 (2001)
4. Ferraiolo, D.F., Sandhu, R., Gavrila, S., Richard, K.D., Chandramouli, R.: Proposed NIST standard for role-based access control. ACM Transactions on Information and System Security 4(3), 224–274 (2001)
5. Koufi, V., Vassilacopoulos, G.: HDGPortal: A Grid Portal Application for Pervasive Access to Process- Based Healthcare Systems. In: Proceedings of the 2nd International Conference in Pervasive Computing Technologies in Healthcare (2008)

6. Hu, J., Weaver, A.C.: A Dynamic, Context-Aware Security Infrastructure for Distributed Healthcare Applications. In: Pervasive Security, Privacy and Trust (PSPT 2004), Boston, MA (August 2004)
7. Sandhu, R., Coyne, E.J., Feinstein, H.L., Youman, C.E.: Role based access control models. IEEE Computer (1996)
8. Smith, H.: A Context-Based Access Control Model for HIPAA Privacy and Security Compliance. In: CISSP (2001)
9. Abawajy, J.H.: Context-based Access Control Mechanism for E-Health Systems, Deakin University, Technical Report (October 2008)
10. Bertino, E., Bonatti, P.A., Ferrari, E.: TRBAC: A Temporal Role-based Access Control Model. ACM Transactions on Information and System Security 4(4) (2001)
11. Joshi, J.B.D., Bertino, E., Latif, U., Ghafoor, A.: Generalized Temporal Role Based Access Control Model (GTRBAC) (Part I)– Specification and Modeling. CERIAS TR 2001-47, Purdue University, USA (2001)
12. Al-Nayadi, F., Abawajy, J.H.: An Authorization Policy Management Framework for Dynamic Medical Data Sharing. In: Proceedings of the IEEE International Conference on Intelligent Pervasive Computing, pp. 313–318 (2007)
13. What is HL7?, Health Level Seven, Inc. (2004), http://www.hl7.org/about/hl7about.htm (retrieved February 6, 2008)
14. Al-Naydi, F., Abawajy, J.H., Deris, M.M.: A Conceptual Framework for Ubiquitously Sharing Heterogeneous Patient Information among Autonomous Healthcare Providers. In: MUE 2007, pp. 299–306 (2007)
15. Al-Naydi, F., Jemal, A.: Authorization policy management framework for dynamic medical data sharing. In: IPC 2007 proceedings: the 2007 International Conference on Intelligent Pervasive Computing, pp. 313–318. IEEE Computer Society, Los Alamitos (2007)

Analysis of a Mathematical Model for Worm Virus Propagation

Wang Shaojie and Liu Qiming

Department of Mathematics, Shijiazhuang Mechanical Engineering College,
Shijiazhuang 050003, China
solgen2008@126.com, lqmmath@yahoo.com.cn

Abstract. Considering the characteristics of the propagation of worm, we can analyze it by epidemic model. In this paper, we build a SIQR model for Internet worm virus propagation depended on the two-factor model. By using the theory of differential equations, the dynamical properties of the model is analyzed, the regularity of Internet worm virus propagation is gained and numerical simulation is presented. The analysis techniques of the mathematical model provide theoretical foundation of control and forecast for Internet worm.

1 Introduction

Recently, computer worms have become a major problem for the security of computer networks, causing considerable amount of resources and time to be spent recovering from virulent attacks. Epidemiological models have been used in previous worm studies. These studies have been used in the SIS model and SIR model [1-7]. To understand the characteristics of the spread of Code Red worm, Zou C C Builds a Two-factor model [8]. People have studied how to defend against worm propagation. But this model has not considered the removed hosts can become the susceptible hosts. We will consider this probability in this paper and build a SIQR model. By using the theory of differential equations, the dynamical properties of the model is analyzed and the regularity of Internet worm virus propagation is gained, and numerical simulation is presented.

2 Mathematical Modeling

2.1 SI Model

At the beginning of a worm outbreak, every system in the given population sample (Internet) is susceptible to the outbreak if they posses exploitable vulnerability, and network worms infect hosts by a startling speed. So the differential equation model is

$$\begin{cases} \dfrac{dI}{dt} = \beta I \\ S + I = N \end{cases} \tag{1}$$

J.H. Park et al. (Eds.): ISA 2009, CCIS 36, pp. 78–84, 2009.
© Springer-Verlag Berlin Heidelberg 2009

Theorem 1. The system (1) has a unique globally asymptotically stable equilibrium $(0, N)$.

From Theorem 1, we can get that $I(t)$ must satisfy $\lim_{t \to \infty} I(t) = N$. But in fact hardly any worm can infect all the hosts. Thus the system (1) can not fit the worm propagation in the later. In order to describe the behavior of worm propagation in the later, we give some appropriate assumptions as follows.

(1) $Q(t)$ is the number of removed hosts from susceptible hosts at time t., and $R(t)$ is the number of removed hosts from infected hosts at time t.

(2) β is the initial infection rate.

(3) Let $\mu > 0, \lambda > 0$ denote removal rate from $S(t)$ to $Q(t)$ and from $I(t)$ to $R(t)$ respectively.

(4) The exponent $\theta > 1$ is used to adjust the infection rate sensitivity to the number of infectious hosts.

2.2 Two-Factor Model

$$
\begin{cases}
\dfrac{dS}{dt} = -\beta (1-\dfrac{I}{N})^{\theta} SI - \mu S(I+R) \\[2mm]
\dfrac{dI}{dt} = \beta (1-\dfrac{I}{N})^{\theta} SI - \lambda I \\[2mm]
\dfrac{dR}{dt} = \lambda I \\[2mm]
\dfrac{dQ}{dt} = \mu S(I+R)
\end{cases}
\tag{2}
$$

Theorem 2. Given system (2), $\lim_{t \to \infty} I(t) = 0$. That is to say the worm will be cleared up.

The proof of Theorem 2 is simple, we omit it.

From Theorem 2 we know that the worm always will be cleared up. But the two-factor model has not considered that the antitoxic immunity can disappear. So the two-factor model is improved on.

2.3 SIQR Model

Now, we give other appropriate assumptions as follows

(5) Let $0 \le k_1 < 1, 0 \le k_2 < 1$ denote from $Q(t)$ to $S(t)$ and from $R(t)$ to $S(t)$ respectively.

Based on the above hypotheses (1)-(5), we propose a new Two-Factor model for worm propagation (NTF model):

$$\begin{cases} \dfrac{dS}{dt} = -\beta\,(1-\dfrac{I}{N})^\theta SI - \mu S(I+R) + k_1 R + k_2 Q \\[2mm] \dfrac{dI}{dt} = \beta\,(1-\dfrac{I}{N})^\theta SI - \lambda I \\[2mm] \dfrac{dR}{dt} = \lambda I - k_1 R \\[2mm] \dfrac{dQ}{dt} = \mu S(I+R) - k_2 Q \end{cases} \tag{3}$$

Although the two-factor model has been improved in many papers, the model (3) can contain some of them. For example, (a) If $k_2 = 0$, model (3) reduces to the model (6) in [9], and we can obtain the same conclusion with the same method of theorem 3. (b)If $k_1 = k_2 = 0$, model (3) reduces to the model (14) in [8].

Considering system (3), we give the following main results under conditions $0 < k_1 < 1, 0 < k_2 < 1$.

Theorem 3. Given system (3),

(1) If $R_1 \le 1$, system (3) has a unique globally asymptotically stable equilibrium $P_0(N,0,0,0)$;

(2) If $R_1 > 1$, system (3) has two equilibriums. The equilibrium $P_0(N,0,0,0)$ is unstable, and if $\quad (k_1 + k_2)(2\mu k_1 + \mu\lambda + \dfrac{\lambda^2}{N} + \dfrac{\lambda}{N} k_1 k_2 + 2k_2 + 2k_2) > \mu\lambda^2$, the equilibrium $P_1(S^*, I^*, R^*, Q^*)$ is locally asymptotically stable.

Where $R_1 = \beta N / \lambda$, $S^* = \dfrac{\lambda}{\beta(1-\dfrac{I^*}{N})^\theta}$ $R^* = \dfrac{\lambda}{k_1} I^*$ $Q^* = N - S^* - I^* - R^*$ and I^* is one positive solution of the equation

$$\dfrac{\lambda}{\beta(1-\dfrac{I}{N})^\theta}\left(\mu(1+\dfrac{\lambda}{k_1})I + k_2\right) - k_2(1+\dfrac{\lambda}{k_1})I - k_2 N = 0 \tag{4}$$

Proof: It is obvious that there always exists equilibrium $P_0(N,0,0,0)$ of system (3), and there may be one possible equilibrium $P_1(I^*, R^*, Q^*)$ of system (3) in the non-negative cone $T = \{(S,I,R) \in R_+^3 : S+I+R \le N\}$

Let $F(I) = \dfrac{\lambda}{\beta}\left(\mu(1+\dfrac{\lambda}{k_1})I + k_2\right)(1-\dfrac{I}{N})^{-\theta} \ \Box \ G(I) = k_2\left((1+\dfrac{\lambda}{k_1})I + N\right),$

So we can obtain $F'(I) > 0$, $G'(I) > 0$

Since $F(0) = \dfrac{k_2\lambda}{\beta}$, $\lim\limits_{I \to N} F(I) = +\infty$ and $G(0) = k_1 N$, $G(N) = -\dfrac{\lambda k_2}{k_1} N < 0$.

If $R_1 \le 1$, there is no positive point of intersection in the curves $F(I)$ and $G(I)$, so (4) has no positive solution, but if $R_1 > 1$, there is a unique positive point of intersection in the curves $F(I)$ and $G(I)$, which implies that (4) has one unique positive solution. Together with $0 < k_1 < 1, 0 < k_2 < 1$, we can get equilibrium $P_1(S^*, I^*, R^*, Q^*)$, thus the system (2) has two equilibriums $(N,0,0,0)$ 和 (S^*, I^*, R^*, Q^*) under condition $R_1 > 1$.

(1)   Since $S + I + R + Q = N$, then $S = N - I - R - Q$, the system (2) is equivalent to differential system

$$\begin{cases} \dfrac{dI}{dt} = \beta\ (1-\dfrac{I}{N})^\theta (N-I-R-Q)I - \lambda I \\[2mm] \dfrac{dR}{dt} = \lambda I - k_1 R \\[2mm] \dfrac{dQ}{dt} = \mu(N-I-R-Q)(I+R)-k_2 Q \end{cases} \qquad (5)$$

Constructing Lyapunov functional $V(I,R,Q) = I$, and calculating the derivative of V along the system (5), we can obtain $\left.\dfrac{dV}{dt}\right|_{(5)} = [\beta(1-\dfrac{I}{N})^\theta S - \lambda]I \le [\beta N - \lambda - \beta I]I$. If

$R_1 \le 1$, then $\left.\dfrac{dV}{dt}\right|_{(5)} \le -\beta I^2 \le 0$. Notice that $E = \{(I,R,Q) \in D | V'(t) = 0\} = \{I = 0\}$, according to LaSalle invariant principle and the theory of the limitation, we have $\lim\limits_{t \to \infty} I(t) = 0$, which implies equilibrium P_0 is globally asymptotically stable.

(Ⅱ) The Jacobi matrix of the system (3) about $(0,0,0)$ is given by :

$$J_0 = \begin{pmatrix} \beta N - \lambda & 0 & 0 \\ \lambda & -k_1 & 0 \\ \mu N & \mu N & -k_2 \end{pmatrix}$$

We can obtain a characteristic equation $(r+\lambda - \beta N)(r+k_1)(r+k_2) = 0$. If $R_1 > 1$, the characteristic root $r = \beta N - \lambda > 0$, thus the equilibrium P_0 is unstable.

(Ⅲ) The Jacobi Matrix of the system (3) about $P_1(I^*, E^*)$ is given by:

$$J_1 = \begin{pmatrix} -a_1 - a_2 & -a_2 & -a_2 \\ \lambda & -k_1 & 0 \\ a_3 & a_3 & -a_4 - k_2 \end{pmatrix},$$

where $a_1 = -\dfrac{\lambda \theta I^*}{N-I^*}$, $\quad a_2 = -\dfrac{\lambda I^*}{N-I^*-R^*-Q^*}$, $\quad a_3 = \mu\left(N-2I^*-2R^*-Q^*\right)$

$,a_4 = \mu\left(I^*+R^*\right)$. Denote $\lambda^3 + c_2\lambda^2 + c_1\lambda + c_0 = 0$ as the characteristic equation

about $P_1(I^*,E^*,Q^*)$, then it is easy to verify that $c_2 > 0, c_1 > 0$ and $c_0 > 0$. Furthermore,

if $(k_1+k_2)(2\mu k_1 + \mu\lambda + \dfrac{\lambda^2}{N} + \dfrac{\lambda}{N}k_1k_2 + 2k_2 + 2k_2) > \mu\lambda^2$ holds, $c_2c_1 - c_0 > 0$. Thus the

equilibrium P_1 is locally asymptotically stable.

Remark: (a) If $k_1 = k_2 = 0$, then $\lim\limits_{x\to\infty} I(t) = 0$ (see Theorem2). (b) If $k_2 = 0, k_1 \neq 0$ or

$k_1 = 0, k_2 \neq 0$, we also obtain that if $R_1 \leq 1$, then $\lim\limits_{t\to\infty} I(t) = 0$.

3 Simulation

(1) Let $N = 500000, I_0 = 100, \beta = 0.00001$, $\theta = 2$, $k_1 = 0.1$, $k_2 = 0.15, \mu = 0.1, \lambda = 0.6$,

where $R_1 < 1$ .We can see the result in Fig. 1.

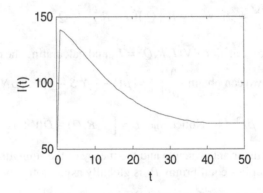

Fig. 1. The number of infected

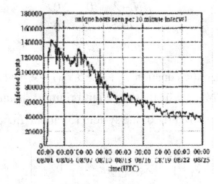

Fig. 2. Infected hosts by Code Red [10]

From our recorded data in Fig.1 and Fig.2, we know countermeasures have not been widely known and distributed at the early stages of a worm incident; the worm was spreading very fast. When the users have woken up to the harm of the worm and effective countermeasures have been taken, the number of infected hosts reduces. Due to $R_1 > 1$, the number of infected hosts I(t) tends to a certain value. In fact the positive equilibrium of system (2) is globally stable, so endemic appear. In order to checkout the validity of the system (2), we compare the result of simulation and the number of Infected hosts by Code Red in CAIDA, and find that the system (2) can describe the propagation of the Code-Red II preferably.

(2) Let $N = 500000, I_0 = 100, \beta = 0.00001, \theta = 2$

$k_1 = 0.1, k_2 = 0.15, \mu = 0.1, \lambda = 0.6$, where $R_1 < 1$. The result of numerical simulation is presented in Fig. 3.

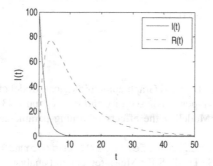

Fig. 3. Comparing I(t), and R(t)

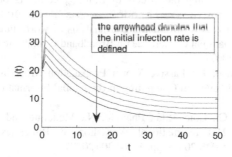

Fig. 4. Influence of the number of infected hosts when β is Changed

(3)Let $N = 500000, I_0 = 100, \beta_1 = 0.000002$ $\beta_2 = 0.000003$, $\beta_3 = 0.000004$, $\beta_4 = 0.000005$, $\beta_5 = 0.000006$, $\theta = 2$ $k_1 = 0.1$, $k_2 = 0.15, \mu = 0.1, \lambda = 0.2$, and let us see the result in Fig. 4. The endemic appear when β is defined with these numbers, and the more increase of β, the more severe of the endemic, and the number of the infected hosts. So it is helpful for the attracters to take effective countermeasures to increase the infected rate β.

4 Conclusion

From theorem 3, we know the threshold is $R_1 = \beta N / \lambda$. If the sample population N is a constant, we always hope to reduce β, and increase λ to make worm cleared up. We also know that if the threshold $R_1 > 1$, that is $\beta N > \lambda$, the number of infected hosts will not go to zero, the worm will not be cleared up.

If we evaluate the parameters in system (3) different values of calculation, we can find that if the condition $R_1 > 1$ is obtained, $I(t)$ will go to a positive value. So we guess if $R_1 > 1$, the equilibrium $P_1(S^*, I^*, R^*, Q^*)$ of system (3) is globally asymptotically stable. We will prove it in the future.

References

1. Kephart, J.O., White, S.R.: Directed Graph epidemiological Model of Computer Viruses. In: Proc. of the 1991 IEEE Symposium on security and Privacy, pp. 343–359 (1991)
2. Wang, Y., Wang, C.X.: Modeling the effects of timing parameters on virus propagation [EB/OL],
   http://xys.ccert.edu.cn/reference/Worms/Worm2003/p61-wang.pdf
3. Kim, J., Radhakrishnan, S., Dhall, S.K.: Measurement and analysis of worm propagation on Internet network topology. In: Proceedings of 13th International Conference on Computer Communications and Networks, pp. 495–500 (2004)
4. Wang, Y., Wang, C.: Modeling the effects of timing parameters on virus propagation,
   http://xys.ccert.edu.cn/reference/Worms/Worm2003/p61-wang.pdf
5. Tanachaiwiwat, S., Helmy, A.X.: Modeling and analysis of worm interactions (war of the worms). In: Fourth International Conference on Broadband Communications, Networks and Systems, pp. 649–658 (2007)
6. Zhou, H., Wen, Y., Zhao, H.: Passive Worm Propagation Modeling and Analysis. In: International Multi-Conference on Computing in the Global Information Technology, p. 32 (2007)
7. Abdelhafez, M., Riley, G., Cole, R.G., Phamdo, N.: Modeling and Simulations of TCP MANET Worms. In: 21st International Workshop on Principles of Advanced and Distributed Simulation (PADS 2007), pp. 123–130 (2007)
8. Zou, C.C., Gong, W., Towsley, D.: Code Red worm propagationmodeling and analysis. In: Proc. of the 9th ACM Symp. on Computer and Communication Security, Washington, pp. 138–147 (2002)
9. Yu, D., Jiwen, Z.: Improved Two-factor worm propagation model. Microcomputer information 26 (2005)

A Contents Encryption Mechanism Using Reused Key in IPTV[*]

Yoon-Su Jeong[1], Yong-Tae Kim[2], Young-Bok Cho[1], Ki-Jeong Lee[2],
Gil-Cheol Park[2,**], and Sang-Ho Lee[3]

[1] Department of Computer Science, Chungbuk National University,
Cheongju, Chungbuk, Korea
{bukmunro,bogi0118}@gmail.com
[2] Department of Multimedia, Hannam University, Daejeon, Chungnam, Korea
{ky7762,gcpark}@hannam.ac.kr, rlwjd@nate.com
[3] School of Electrical & Computer Engineering, Chungbuk National University,
Cheongju, Chungbuk, Korea
shlee@chungbuk.ac.kr

Abstract. Recently IPTV is being spotlighted as a new stream service
to stably provide video, audio and control signals to subscribers through
the application of IP protocol. However, the IPTV system is facing more
security threats than the traditional TV. This study proposes a multicasting encryption mechanism for secure transmission of the contents of
IPTV by which the content provider encrypts their contents and send
the encrypted contents and the key used for encryption of the contents to
the user. In order to reduce the time and cost of Head-End, the proposed
mechanism encrypts the media contents at the Head-End, embeds the
code of the IPTV terminal used at the Head-End in the media contents
for user tracking, and performs desynchronization for protection of the
media contents from various attacks.

1   Introduction

IPTV provides subscribers with entertainment video-related services by applying
the IP protocol to stably send video, audio and control signals to the subscribers,
and sends streamed visual contents through a managed IP network with guaran-
teed QoS to the TV or similar devices of subscribers [2]. However, the IPTV system is facing more security threats than the traditional TV. For example, when
the user privacy is compromised in a larger area, the system can be more vulnerable to the DoS (Denial of Service) attack. Even though some DRM (Digital
Rights Management) systems have been proposed to protect general multimedia
services, it cannot solve the security issues of IPTV alone.

Research of Conditional Access (CA) in IPTV is still in its infancy. Recently,
Park et al.[4] proposed a contents distribution system based on MPEG-4 IS-
MACryp in the IP set-top box (STB) to run a safe DRM client in a set-top box.

---

[*] This work was supported by the Security Engineering Research Center, granted by
the Korea Ministry of Knowledge Economy.
[**] Corresponding author.

J.H. Park et al. (Eds.): ISA 2009, CCIS 36, pp. 85–90, 2009.
© Springer-Verlag Berlin Heidelberg 2009

Wang et al.[5] proposed a software update technique for IPTV STB to create an IP STB for IPTV which can prevent update failure. Lin and Chen[6] proposed an STB control technique by a mobile device as an example of the convergence between TV and mobile system. Psecador et al.[7] proposed the performance of DSP by IPTV for low-cost services.

The development of IPTV services requires STBs with high efficiency and encrypted TV programs face the problem of information leakage in the space between STB and TV set. This paper proposes a multicasting encryption mechanism for secure transmission of the contents of IPTV by which the content provider encrypts their contents and send the encrypted contents and the key used for encryption of the contents to the user. The proposed mechanism reuses the key to provide the integrity and confidentiality of contents when they are redistributed to other IPTV terminals while reducing the overhead of Head-End and IPTV terminals. The reused key is created through the key establishment process, and the user's key is used for the confidentiality and authentication of data traffic in the key establishment process.

The remainder of this paper is organized as follows. Section 2 analyzes the past studies on IPTV security. Section 3 presents multicasting encryption mechanism by which contents providers encrypt contents using a reused key and safely send it to the user. Section 4 analyzes the performance of the proposed mechanism in comparison to existing techniques. Finally, Section 5 summarizes the results of this paper and suggests the direction of future studies.

2   Related Works

Lee proposed a key distribution scheme for CAS based on the four level hierarchy: Control Word (CW), Direct Entitlement Key (DEK), Distribution Key (DK), and Master Private Key (MPK). CW and DEK has the same functions as the Control Word and Authorize Key (AK) defined in ITU-R 810. The Lee scheme encrypts the n-1 level key by the n level key (encryption of CW by DEK, DEK by DK, and DK by MPK). The Lee scheme is appropriate if the service provider uploads private and public keys through a secure module, but its weakness is the generation of high communication load during the communication process.

Tu et al. proposed a four-level scheme in which the DK in the Lee scheme is replaced with RGK. In the Tu et al. scheme, the subscribers form different reception groups and change groups according to their channels and payments of rates during a specific period. RGK is assigned to differentiate the received groups along with the groups whose rates have been collected, and a cross-referenced model of many small groups is formed. In the event that payment of rates begins on a specific date, the Tu et al. scheme offers the advantage of distributing keys to all days of one month and sharing it. However, most consumers cannot join the service within a specific period of a month. In this case, if the distribution key update requires a high volume of package broadcasting, it cannot achieve good performance.

Huang et al. proposed a four-level scheme for subscriber services which consists of CW, AK, DK, and secret key for subscriber. By controlling the delivery and update of AK and DK, the Huang et al. scheme allows service providers to bill on a daily basis instead of monthly basis like traditional broadcasting services. But this scheme offers lower security than other techniques. The reason for this is that because all the authorize keys are closely correlated during the IPTV service, it is easy to calculate them for the services that users with different permissions are using now.

The broadcast encryption [1] and multicast key management [3] techniques which are under research now are being applied for the access control of pay TV systems. To apply these schemes to pay TV, there must be a corresponding group for each channel. As a result, many channels in the system have communication and calculation loads. For the broadcast encryption technique, a key setting value must be given to every user so that the user can be located at a fixed layer.

3 Multicasting Contents Encryption Mechanism Using Reused Key

The proposed mechanism encrypts multicasting contents using a reused key for the following benefits: First, some of the contents of Head-End are encrypted to reduce the time and cost of Head-End. Second, after the IPTV terminal code is embedded in the media contents at Head-End for user tracking, the media contents are desynchronized for higher security. Third, to reuse the key for media contents encryption, the key reuse establishment process is carried out between IPTV terminal and Head-End.

3.1 Media Contents Encryption Using Multicasting

In the media contents encryption using multicasting, IPTV terminals operate in different types. For the IPTV terminals to form groups, the IPTV terminals must periodically update authentication information. To periodically update the authentication information of the IPTV terminals, Head-End must divide contents into n parts and hash the contents in the reverse order to chain the contents. In the proposed mechanism, the random number N is included in the generation of CBC (Ciper Block Code) to prevent the attack of the second preimage. The coded message C1 that has been sent to the IPTV terminal and the prior coded message C0 are calculated from the contents D1 and H2 for verification. K_0 is generated through key reuse establishment process between IPTV terminal and Head-End.

3.2 Key Reuse Establishment Process between IPTV Terminal and Head-End

The proposed mechanism assumes that IPTV terminal and Head-End shares the shared key K_{BSA_1} that has been agreed beforehand between them before Step 1. To create a reused key in Step 1, the random number N_A created by

IPTV terminal and SAI (Secure Authentication Information) are expressed as $\{E_{PK_{BS}}(N_A), MAC_{K_{BSA_1}}(N_A, SAI)\}$ and sent to Head-End. In step 2, Head-End sends the random number N_B that it created and the certificate $Cert_{BS}$ to the IPTV terminal together with the random number N_A sent from the IPTV terminal. Through the received information, the IPTV terminal and Head-End applies the shared key K_{BSA_1} and random numbers (N_A, N_{BS}) to the one-way hash function to create a new shared key K_{BSA_2} between the IPTV terminal and Head-End. Even if an attacker steals the sent/received contents and compromise the key, the newly generated key K_{BSA_2} cannot decrypt the encrypted contents with the initial keys (k-1, k-2, k, ..., k-n) due to the characteristics of the one-way has function. In step 3, the IPTV terminal and Head-End selects two keys (old key(K_{BSA_1}) and new key(K_{BSA_2})) when encrypting or decrypting all messages. The reason for selecting two keys is that the old key K_{BSA_1} may be applied to the MAC() before the key K_{BSA_2} is created between the IPTV terminal and Head-End. In the process of decrypting the received message, step 3 decrypts the received message using the old key first between the two public keys. If it fails, it decrypts the message after replacing the old key with the new key. In step 4, Head-End verifies the certificate $Cert_{BS}$ before decrypting the contents from the IPTV terminal with the new key. Once the verification of the certificate finishes, it decrypts the contents with the new key and deletes the old key. In the process of decrypting the contents, Head-End tries to decrypt the contents using the old key. If it fails, it tries to decrypt new contents using the new key. During the time when the old key is deleted in step 4, an average delay occurs in the link due to the characteristics of wireless equipment. In step 5, contents are sent between IPTV terminal and Head-End using the new key K_{BSA_2}.

3.3 Establishment of a Group Key of Head-End

This section describes the process in which the Head-End establishes a group key for multicasting with IPTV terminals to form a communication group between IPTV terminals located in the communication range of Head-End. To distribute the group key, the Head-End encrypts the group key with the shared key K_{BSA} between the IPTV terminal and Head-End created in section 3.2. The Head-End creates the group key GK_{AB} to send to the desired IPTV terminal, encrypts it with the keys K_{BSA} and K_{BSB} shared with IPTV terminals together with the random number , and distributes it to the IPTV terminals. The IPTV terminal decrypts the group key using the keys K_{BSA} and K_{BSB} shared with the Head-End, and sends the identifier of the IPTV terminal to the Head-End using HMAC together with the random number N_{BS} using the group key. Finally, the IPTV terminal analyzes the received HMAC value and verifies that it accurately possesses the group key GK_{AB}.

4   Performance Evaluation

Figure 1 compares the key encryption overhead by number of subscribers of the proposed scheme with the those of the Lee scheme, Tu et al. scheme, and

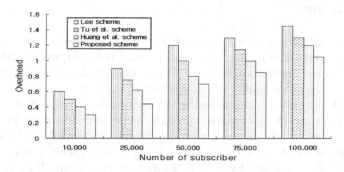

Fig. 1. Key Encryption Overhead by Number of Subscribers

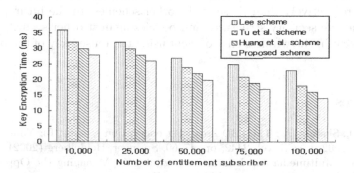

Fig. 2. Key Encryption Time of Entitlement Subscribers

Huang et al. scheme. The encryption overhead of the proposed scheme was evaluated to be lower than the Lee scheme, Tu et al. scheme, and Huang et al. scheme even when the number of subscribers increased. The reason for this is that a hash function of the signature type was used when the data are encrypted by the proposed protocol to generate lower encryption overhead compared to other public key-based encryption algorithms used in the other schemes. The evaluation of the key encryption overhead by the number of subscribers found that the proposed scheme showed overheads lower by 8.9%, 12.3%, and 16% on average than the Lee scheme, Tu et al. scheme, and Huang et al. scheme, respectively.

Figure 2 compares the key encryption time of the entitlement key by the number of subscribers of the proposed scheme with those of the Lee scheme, Tu et al. scheme, and Huang et al. scheme. The key encryption time of the proposed scheme was lower than that of the Lee scheme, Tu et al. scheme, and Huang et al. scheme even when the number of subscribers increased rapidly because it did not use the public key encryption method like the other schemes did and applied the identifier and password of smart card that was registered during the registration process using the hash function of the signature type to the authentication and maintenance processes. In particular, the key encryption time of the proposed scheme was shorter by 4%, 6.9%, and 8.5% on average than those of the Lee scheme, Tu et al. scheme, and Huang et al. scheme.

5   Conclusion

In this paper, we proposed a multicasting encryption mechanism for content providers to encrypt the contents and safely send the encrypted contents and the key used for the encryption to users. The proposed scheme reuses the key for the integrity and confidentiality of contents when the contents are redistributed to other IPTV terminals while reducing the overheads of Head-End and IPTV terminals. This reused key is created through the key establishment process and the user's key used in the key reuse establishment process offers the confidentiality and authentication of data traffic. The key encryption overhead of the proposed scheme was lower by 8.9%, 12.3%, and 16% than those of the Lee scheme, Tu et al. scheme, and Huang et al. scheme, respectively. The subscriber key encryption time of the proposed scheme was shorter by 4%, 6.9%, and 8.5% on average respectively than those of the other schemes. In the future, we plan to study the safe security structures and policies against other security attacks that may occur in the wireless environment using the reused key of the proposed scheme.

References

1. Halevy, D., Shamir, A.: The LSD broadcast encryption scheme. In: Yung, M. (ed.) CRYPTO 2002. LNCS, vol. 2442, pp. 47–60. Springer, Heidelberg (2002)
2. Pagani, M.: Multimedia and Interactive Digital TV - Managing the Opportunities Created by Digital Convergence. IRM Press (2003)
3. Sherman, A.T., McGrew, D.A.: Key establishment in large dynamic groups using one-way functions trees. IEEE Trans. Softw. Eng. 29(5), 444–458 (2003)
4. Park, S., Jeong, J., Kwon, T.: Contents Distribution System Based on MPEG-4 ISMACryp in IP Set-top Box Environments. IEEE Transactions on Consumer Electronics 52(2) (May 2006)
5. Wang, Q., Du, Q., Lin, G.: IPTV STB Software Update Scheme Based on SNMP. In: 2006 IEEE International Conference on Electro/information Technology, 197–200 (May 2006)
6. Lin, C.-C., Chen, M.-S.: On Controlling Digital TV Set-Top-Box by Mobile Devices via IP Network. In: Proceedings of the Seventh IEEE International Symposium on Multimedia (ISM 2005) (2005)
7. Pescador, F., Sanz, C., Garrido, M.J., Santos, C., Antoniello, R.: A DSP Based IP Set-Top Box for Home Entertainment. IEEE Transactions on Consumer Electronics 52(1) (February 2006)

High Capacity Method for Real-Time Audio Data Hiding Using the FFT Transform

Mehdi Fallahpour and David Megías

Estudis d'Informàtica, Multimèdia i Telecomunicació,
Universitat Oberta de Catalunya- Rambla del Poblenou, 156, Barcelona, Spain
Tel.: (+34) 933 263 600; Fax: (+34) 933 568 822
{mfallahpour,dmegias}@uoc.edu

Abstract. This paper presents a very efficient method for audio data hiding which is suitable for real-time applications. The FFT magnitudes which are in a band of frequencies between 5 and 15 kHz are modified slightly and the frequencies which have a magnitude less than a threshold are used for embedding. Its low complexity is one of the most important properties of this method making it appropriate for real-time applications. In addition, the suggested scheme is blind, since it does not need the original signal for extracting the hidden bits. The Experimental results show that it has a very good capacity (5 kbps), without significant perceptual distortion and provides robustness against MPEG compression (MP3).

Keywords: Audio data hiding, Fast Fourier Transform (FFT), Real time.

1 Introduction

By the growth of audio production and broadcasting, security issues have arisen for audio producers. Recently, watermarking has been suggested as a good means for protecting audio against illegal tasks mainly for ownership proof and copy/modification detection. While most multimedia watermarking researches have been devoted to images so far, in the last decade many audio watermarking schemes have been suggested. These methods use the weakness of the human auditory system to embed the hidden data in the regions of the audio signals at which human ears are unable to perceive the distortion caused by the data embedding process.

Considering the embedding domain, audio watermarking techniques can be classified into time domain and frequency domain methods. In time domain schemes, the hidden bits are embedded directly into the time signal samples. These methods are easy to implement and are usually very efficient but they tend to be weak against common signal processing attacks. Phase modulation [1] and echo hiding [2] are well known methods in the time domain.

In frequency domain watermarking, after taking one of the usual transforms such as FFT, MDCT and WT from the signal, the hidden bits are embedded into the resulting transform coefficients [3-6]. In [6] the low-frequency coefficients of the wavelet transform are used for embedding the watermark. The robustness of this

J.H. Park et al. (Eds.): ISA 2009, CCIS 36, pp. 91–97, 2009.
© Springer-Verlag Berlin Heidelberg 2009

scheme against various attacks is high but this method is not adaptive. Consequently, this scheme cannot be used in real-time software and users have to determine the embedding strength by using subjective audio quality tests for each audio signal. This process is very time-consuming and costly. In other group of schemes, the hidden data are embedded into the audio signal by changing middle frequency components in the frequency domain [7] or in the time domain [8].

Using methods based on transforms provides a better perception quality and robustness against common attacks at the price of increasing the computational complexity. For real-time applications complexity is the most important issue to be considered. In [9], an efficient audio watermarking method suitable for real-time applications is proposed. In this method, the hidden bits are embedded into the scale factor values during the MP3 encoding process. Also, [10] proposes a method to embed and extract the watermarks into and from digital compressed audio and therefore is applicable only to compressed audio. J. Garcia [11] proposed a real-time method which use spread spectrum algorithm in the modulated complex lapped transform (MCLT) domain to embed the watermark. In fact, just a few algorithms for an efficient real-time audio watermarking have been proposed so far.

In this paper we present a very efficient method for audio watermarking which is suitable for real-time applications. This scheme has been implemented taking special care for the efficient usage of the two restricted resources of computer systems: memory space and CPU time. It offers to the industrial user the capability of watermark embedding and detection in time immediately comparable to the real playing time of the original audio file, while the end user/audience does not find any artifacts or delays hearing the watermarked audio file. In the proposed algorithm, the FFT magnitudes of the selected clip which are in a band of frequency between 5 and 15 kHz are slightly distorted and magnitudes which have a value lower than a chosen threshold are used for embedding. This frequency band is scanned and when we meet the magnitude with the value lower the threshold it is increased if the corresponding embedding bit is '1', otherwise the magnitude is not altered.

Low complexity is one of the most important properties of this method, making it appropriate for real-time applications. In addition, the suggested scheme is blind one since it does not need the original signal for extracting the hidden bits. The experimental results show that the method has a very high capacity (above 5 kbps) and provides robustness against MPEG compression.

The rest of the paper is organised as follows. In Section 2 the suggested scheme is presented. In Section 3, the experimental results are shown. Finally, Section 4 summarises the most relevant conclusions of this research.

2 Suggested Scheme

We have chosen the Fast Fourier transform (FFT) domain to embed the hidden data to exploit the translation-invariant property of the FFT transform such that small distortions in the time domain can be resisted. Compared to other schemes, such as quantisation or odd/even modulation, keeping the relationship of FFT coefficient pairs is a more realistic scheme under distortions. We select a band of frequency between 5 kHz and 15 kHz to embed the data, choosing the frequencies for which the value of the magnitude is near one. Since we need integer values for the FFT magnitude in the embedding step, these magnitudes are multiplied by a reference level q and then rounded to the nearest integer. This scaling and rounding process generates a great deal of zero values in the magnitudes, so the signal will result slightly distorted. Changing the parameter q, both the capacity and the perceptual distortion will be affected. When q decreases, the capacity is increased but the perceptual distortion also enlarges and vice versa (capacity and distortion can decrease by rising q).

Figure 1 shows an example of selecting a band to embed data. The experimental results presented in Section 3 show how this choice affects the properties of the watermarking scheme (capacity and transparency). The choice of the band of frequencies and the reference level q depends on the application. For example, if the marked audio should have a very high capacity a wide frequency band could be selected but this would increase distortion.

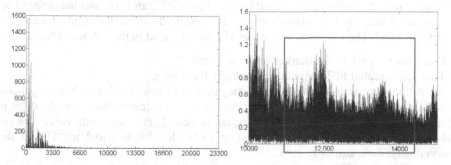

Fig. 1. (a) Magnitude of the spectrum for the violoncello wave file and (b) selected band for embedding

The watermarking scheme presented here is positional. This means that the detector must be synchronised in order to recover the embedded bits correctly. In a real application, the cover signal would be divided into several blocks of a few seconds and it is essential that the detector can determine the position (the beginning sample) of each of these blocks. One of the most practical solutions to solve this problem is to use synchronisation marks such that the detector can determine the beginning of each block. Several synchronisations strategies have been described in the literature (for example [15, 16]) and any of them could be used together with the method described here in order to produce a practical self-synchronising solution.

The embedding and detection methods are described in the following sections.

2.1 Watermark Embedding

The embedding steps are as follows:

1- Based on the computation processor (speed and memory) select the length of the segment of the audio file.
2- Calculate the FFT of the audio segment.
3- Select the band of frequencies between 5 kHz and 15 kHz for which the magnitudes are near 1.

4- Using q as a parameter, convert the FFT magnitudes to integer values (multiplying them by q and then rounding).

5- Expanding step: scan all these integer FFT magnitudes in the selected band. If a magnitude is larger than zero then increase it by 1. After this step we have no magnitude with the value 1.

6- Embedding step: scan again all integer FFT magnitudes in selected band. When a zero magnitude is found, if the corresponding embedded bit is '1' add one to the magnitude. Otherwise, the magnitude is not changed. After this step all magnitudes with value zero or one represent an embedded bit.

7- The marked (FFT) signal is achieved by dividing all the magnitudes by q.

8- Finally, use IFFT to achieve the marked audio segment in the time domain.

2.2 Watermark Extracting

The watermark detection is performed by using the FFT transform and the embedding parameters. Since the host audio signal is not required in the detection process, the detector is blind. The detection process can be summarised in the following steps:

1- Calculate the FFT of the marked audio segment.

2- To achieve scaled FFT magnitudes multiply them by q.

3- Detection step: scan all scaled FFT magnitudes in selected band. If a magnitude with value in the interval [0, 1/2) is found, then the corresponding embedded bit is equal to '0' and the restored magnitude equals to zero. If the magnitude value is in the interval [1/2, 3/2), then the corresponding embedded bit is equal to '1' and the restored magnitude equals to zero.

4- Scan all scaled FFT magnitudes in the selected band. If each magnitude value in interval [k+1/2, k+3/2), then the restored magnitude equals to k.

5- The restored magnitudes are achieved by dividing them by q.

6- Finally, use IFFT to achieve the restored audio segment.

3   Experimental Results

To evaluate the performance of the proposed method, two pieces of audio signals have been selected from the Sound Quality Assessment Material (SQAM) corpus audio files [12], used for watermarking. All audio clips were sampled at 44.1 kHz with 16 bits per sample resolution. The experiments have been performed for each channel of the audio signals separately. Hence, we have four test mono signals.

The Objective Difference Grade (ODG) is used to evaluate the transparency of the proposed algorithm. The ODG is one of the output values of the ITU-R BS.1387 PEAQ [13] standard, and its description is shown in Table 1. Additionally, the software OPERA [14] based on ITU-R BS. 1387 was used to provide an objective measure of quality.

Tables 2, 3, 4, and 5 show the effect of changing the scaling coefficient q and the width of the selected frequency band (B) on capacity, transparency (ODG) and the BER of detection after MPEG compression for the Trumpet (trpt21_2.wav) and Violoncello (vioo10_2.wav) wave files.

Table 1. ODG description

Impairment	ODG
Imperceptible	0.0
perceptible, not annoying	−1.0
slightly annoying	−2.0
Annoying	−3.0
very annoying	−4.0

Table 2. Trumpet.wav left channel

q	Frequency band (kHz)	Capacity (bps)	ODG	Mp3 rate (kbps)	BER %
5	8.5-16	7205	−0.73	128(> 128)	1.0 (0.0)
5	11-16	5038	−0.67	128(> 128)	1.2 (0.0)
4	6.5-16	8454	−0.95	128(> 128)	1.0 (0.0)
4	5-11	6009	−0.92	≥ 128	0.0
3	5-11	6050	−1.71	≥ 128	0.0
3	3-14	7449	−1.94	128	1.7
3	3-14	7449	−1.94	> 128	0.0

Table 3. Trumpet.wav right channel

q	Frequency band (kHz)	Capacity (bps)	ODG	Mp3 rate (kbps)	BER %
5	8.5-16	5860	−0.67	128	1.0
5	11-16	2534	−0.71	128	0.0
4	6.5-16	6083	−0.93	128	1.0
4	5-11	3954	−1.06	≥ 128	0.0
3	5-11	4418	−1.51	≥ 128	0.0
3	3-14	7560	−1.75	128	1.1

Table 4. Violoncello left channel

q	Frequency band (kHz)	Capacity (bps)	ODG	Mp3 rate (kbps)	BER %
1.5	11-14	4074	−1.06	≥ 128	0.0
1.75	11-14	3570	−0.91	128 (> 128)	0.5 (0.0)

Table 5. Violoncello right channel

q	Frequency band (kHz)	Capacity (bps)	ODG	Mp3 rate (kbps)	BER %
1.5	11-14	3155	−0.93	128 (>128)	3.0 (0.0)
1.25	11-14	3788	−1.17	≥ 128	0.0

Table 6. Computation time

Audio File	Time (sec)	Embedding time (sec)	Extracting time (sec)
Violoncello	30	4.15	4.01
Trumpet	17.8	1.82	1.76

In Table 2, the first and second rows show the results obtained with the same q and different B. When using a wider frequency band both the capacity and the perceptual distortion increase. Note that BER is provided for various MPEG compression rates. The fourth and fifth rows show that when q increases, capacity decreases but perceptual distortion is reduced. Finally the sixth and seventh rows show that the BER is affected by the MP3 compression rate.

It is worth to mentioning that Reed-Solomon Codes (or other error correction codes) could be used to improve BER rates if required (at the price of reducing the capacity). Similar results are shown in the other tables.One of important issue in audio watermarking is computation time. As FFT is a fast transform this method is very useful for real-time applications. Table 6 illustrates the embedding and extracting times. It worth to mention that these computation times have been achieved with an Intel (R) core (TM) 2 Duo 2.2GHz CPU and 2 GB of RAM memory. It can be noticed that the extracting time is one order of magnitude smaller than the file playing time. Thus, it is perfectly possible to recover the embedded data in a real-time scenario.

5 Conclusion

In this paper, we describe a high capacity data hiding algorithm for digital audio which is appropriate for real-time applications. A scaling coefficient (q) and the selected frequency band to embed the hidden information in it are the two main parameters of this method. The experimental results show that using different values for q and the frequency band lead to different capacity, perceptual distortion (ODG) and bit error rates (BER) of detection after MP3 compression. Low complexity is one of the most important properties of this method, making it suitable for real time applications. Furthermore, the suggested scheme is blind, since it does not need the original signal for extracting the hidden bits. The experimental results show that this scheme has a very good capacity (5 kbps or above), without significant perceptual distortion and provides robustness against MPEG compression (MP3).

Acknowledgement

This work is partially supported by the Spanish Ministry of Science and Innovation and the FEDER funds under the grants TSI2007-65406-C03-03 E-AEGIS and CONSOLIDER-INGENIO2010 CSD2007-00004 ARES.

References

1. Lie, W.N., Chang, L.C.: Multiple Watermarks for Stereo Audio Signals Using Phase-Modulation Techniques. IEEE Trans. Signal Processing 53(2), 806–815 (2005)
2. Kim, H.J., Choi, Y.H.: A novel echo hiding scheme with backward and forward kernels. IEEE Trans. Circuit and Systems, 885–889 (August 2003)
3. Esmaili, S., Krishnan, S., Raahemifar, K.: A novel spread spectrum audio watermarking scheme based on time - frequency characteristics. In: IEEE Conf. Electrical and Computer Engineering, vol. 3, pp. 1963–1966 (May 2003)
4. Megías, D., Herrera-Joancomartí, J., Minguillón, J.: A robust audio watermarking scheme based on MPEG 1 layer 3 compression. In: Lioy, A., Mazzocchi, D. (eds.) CMS 2003. LNCS, vol. 2828, pp. 226–238. Springer, Heidelberg (2003)
5. Sriyingyong, N., Attakitmongcol, K.: Wavelet-Based Audio Watermarking Using Adaptive Tabu Search. In: IEEE Int. Symp. Wireless Pervasive Computing, pp. 1–5 (January 2006)
6. Wu, S., Huang, J., Huang, D., Shi, Y.Q.: Efficiently Self-Synchronized Audio Watermarking for Assured Audio Data Transmission. IEEE Trans. Broadcasting 51(1), 69–76 (2005)
7. Li, W., Xue, X., Lu, P.: Localized Audio Watermarking Technique Robust Against Time-Scale Modification. IEEE Trans. Multimedia 8(1), 60–69 (2006)
8. Lemma, A.N., Aprea, J., Oomen, W., Kerkhof, L.v.d.: A Temporal Domain Audio Watermarking Technique. IEEE Trans. signal processing 51(4), 1088–1097 (2003)
9. Koukopoulos, D., Stamatiou, Y.: An Efficient WatermarkingMethod for MP3 Audio Files., Transaction on Engineering, Computer and Technology V7 (August 2005)
10. Xu, C., Zhu, Y., Feng, D.D.: A robust and fast watermarking scheme for compressed audio. In: IEEE International Conference on Multimedia and Expo (2001) ISBN 0-7695-1198-8/01
11. Garcia, J., Nakano, M., Perez, H.: Real time implementation of low complexity audio watermarking algorithm. In: Proc. Third International Workshop on Random Fields and Processing in Inhomogeneous Media (October 2005)
12. SQAM Sound Quality Assessment Material,
    http://sound.media.mit.edu/mpeg4/audio/sqam/
13. Thiede, T., Treurniet, W.C., Bitto, R., Schmidmer, C., Sporer, T., Beerens, J.G., Colomes, C., Keyhl, M., Stoll, G., Brandenburg, K., Feiten, B.: PEAQ - The ITU Standard for Objective Measurement of Perceived Audio Quality. Journal of the AES 48(1/2), 3–29 (2000)
14. OPTICOM OPERA software site,
    http://www.opticom.de/products/configurations.html
15. Wang, X.-Y., Zhao, H.: A novel synchronization invariant audio watermarking scheme based on DWT and DCT. IEEE Transactions on Signal Processing 54(12), 4835–4840 (2006)
16. Lin, Y., Abdulla, W.: A secure and robust audio watermarking scheme using multiple scrambling and adaptive synchronization. In: Proceedings of the 6th International Conference on Information, Communications & Signal Processing, pp. 1–5 (2007)

Experiment Research of Automatic Deception Model Based on Autonomic Computing[*]

Bingyang Li, Huiqiang Wang, and Guangsheng Feng

College of Computer Science and Technology, Harbin Engineering University
libingyang@hrbeu.edu.cn

Abstract. Aiming at the fact that the network deception technology needs manual work and can't ensure deception efficiency and accuracy, an automatic deception system with autonomic intrusion tolerance based on autonomic computing is proposed. The theory model of the system is researched and the formal description is denoted which includes service transplant module and decoy subnet module. Service transplant module completes the retargeting of suspicious information and recovering of legal access, implementing the security isolation for object system and inputting deception targets to decoy subnet. Trapping subnet realizes automatic deception, feature analysis and autonomic associative study on attack information. The simulation results show the service availability, even response time, average delay, even transmission speed and resource efficiency of the servers with automatic deception are much better than those of servers without automatic deception.

Keywords: Autonomic Intrusion Tolerance; Automatic Deception; Service Transplant; Associative learning.

1 Introduction

With the rapid popularization and development of internet, the complexity, scale and speed of network system are increasing quickly, and the risks brought by its opening and security vulnerability exist all the time, the security problems have been the important strategic subject related to the national stability and social development. Intrusion tolerant technology is the main representative of the third generation information security technology whose main thought is tolerance, as his core, the deception technique has been the a main directions in fields of network security.[1]

There are many organizations are researching and discussing the networked trap and entrapment technology, some companies have introduced some related productions, academia research the network trap and entrapment systems mainly, such as Honeypot. Honeypot is a kind of safety resources, its value is been detected, attacked [1], no matter how can we dispose it, Our objective is let it be detected, attacked and intruded.

---

[*] This paper is supported by The National High Technology Research and Development Program of China (863) (2007AA01Z401), The National Natural Science Foundation of China (90718003).

J.H. Park et al. (Eds.): ISA 2009, CCIS 36, pp. 98–104, 2009.

Honeypot is not a solution, oppositely it is a tool, and how to use this tool depends on the result you want to get. " Cuckoos Egg"[2] the book wrote by Cliff Stoll and "An Evening with Berferd"[3] wrote by Bill Cheswick has mentioned the concept of Honeypot. An organization in America studys Honeynet specially[4]; they devote to know the tool, policy and notivation used by hacker and the knowledge hold by hacker. Marty Roesch who is the founder of Snort and Symantec's Brian Hemacki have classified Honeypot from different sides. The related research has risks as below: (1) service performance of system descends or loses when trapping; (2) manager can't control network entrapment systems; (3) hurting the nomal service request. So using the networked trap need manager input, it enhances the complexity of network management. How to avoid the danger, nomitor and manage the system and analysis in time make the use of network entrapment systems more complex, and can't guarantee the efficiency and accuracy of trapping. This paper proposed an automatic deception system with autonomic intrusion tolerance based on autonomic computing, and made the research of the modeling of theory and data and experiment simulations.

2 Automatic Deception Conceptual Model

Autonomic computing(AC) is firstly presented by Paul Horn in 2001. IT is inspired from the autonomic nervous system of human body [5]. Its basic idea is designing a self-aware, self-management distributed computer system, which completely hides its complexity and provides the user with an interface meets her/his needs [6-9].

2.1 Model Structure

In order to avoid suspicious information to attack target system, system must cut off the access before the intruders perceive and analyze and identify the information of the intruders, thereby it can offer the credible input for excute module to realize intrusion tolerance for suspicious information. The work principle of automatic deception model is shown in Figure 1.

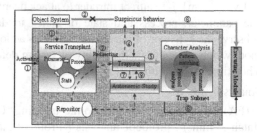

Fig. 1. Automatic Deception Model

2.2 Service Transplant

When suspicious information appear, service transplant function can transplant suspicious access to trap subnet, and cut off the access of suspicious information to target system in time, and recover access of normal information to object system.

(1) Retarget of suspicious information. Aiming at service request of suspicious information (Suspicious Request, SR), service transplant module transplants the service Parameters (Parameters in Object, pao), process (Process in Object, pro) and state (State in Object, sto) of the object system to trap subnet dynamically to accomplish the retarget of object system (Retargeting, r) . It is obvious that process of the transplant is mapping function from service request of suspicious information to retargeting service request. We use logical value 0 denotes the disconnection of suspicious information to access object system (Access to Object, AtO) and 1 denotes the connection. When services are transplanted, system need cut off the access of suspicious information in time, namely setting $AtO = 0$, thereby protect the safety of operation process, and enhance the ability of intrusion tolerance.

(2) Recover credible information access. After characteristic analysis are over in trap subnet and judge trapped information are normal connection. Service transplant module accomplishes the inverse process of retargeting operation, at one time the access of normal information to the object system is recovered to $AtO = 1$

2.3 Trapping Subnet

On the basis of trapping network concept of intrusion behavior redirection type, this paper simulated a relative independent trapping subnet, whose major function is to carry on the service function of object system (O') , autonomous deception of intrusion behavior (Autonomic Study , AS) , matching analysis (Feature Analysis, FA) of intrusion character and autonomic study (Autonomic Study , AS) of intrusion character. So trapping subnet TN= O'+ AD + FA + AS. The four functions are interinhibitive exist.

(1) Automatic Trapping

After trapping subnets received service request of suspicious information, they judge them as intrusion information, combine intrusion records (Intrusion Records , IR={ir1, ir2,…, irn})   in intrusion knowledge database, show many Vulnerabilities (Vulnerability, V={v1,v2,…, vm}) to attract intruder to attack deeply, through tracking it they can update the parameter, process and state of attack to definitude its attack intention. And it can observe the behavior of intruder and note its action, analyze its level, motive, tool and method, which can enhance the ability of system defense. This can help implement module to buy time to deal with this kind of attack.

(2) Character Analysis

Character analysis(FA) can expand with autonomic trapping, Here we use mode matching (Mode Match , mm) , protocol analysis (Protocol Analysis , pa) and command parsing (Command Parsing, cp) to analyze characters. So FA= {mm, pa, cp}. Pattern matching can find suspicious action through checking and analyzing the characters of certain attack in network data packet. Combined with catching high speed data packet, protocol analysis and order resolving are used to analyze known communication protocol structure to deal with data frames, thereby distinguishing the true intention of communication behavior.

(3) Autonomic Associative Study.

If the result of the character analysis shows this access is once malicious attack, then the intrusion character will be correlated (Correlation , c1) , compared (Comparing , c2) and integrated analysis with the former intrusion state record in intrusion knowledge base to find the rule of the forming and developing of the safety hidden trouble, and forecast the production condition of hidden trouble and the early symptom of hidden trouble, adopting the method of diagnosing forecast and intelligent decision-making to implement the autonomic associative learning, and input the result of learning into intrusion data-base.

3 Mathematical Model of Autonomic Trap

According to suspicious information retargeting of service transplant module and formal description of the recover of credible information access and timing relationship of its response, function of service transplant module can be described as:

$$SR \Rightarrow \begin{cases} pa_o \xrightarrow[\overline{t'(pa_o),AtO=1}]{t(pa_o),AtO=0} pa_r \\ pr_o \xrightarrow[\overline{t'(pr_o),AtO=1}]{t(pr_o),AtO=0} pr_r \\ st_o \xrightarrow[\overline{t'(st_o),AtO=1}]{t(st_o),AtO=0} st_r \end{cases} \Rightarrow SR_r$$

Combines the autonomic trap, character analysis and the functional description of the autonomic associative learning of the trap subnet, the coupling relationship of trapping time sequence of trap subnet can be described as:

The relation of safety time sequence of each link in autonomic trapping architecture is clarity, base on the causality and timing relationship among functional description of the theory of autonomic trapping system and formal description of each module, according to the retarget of suspicious information, recovery of credible information's access, autonomic trapping, character analysis and autonomic associative learning, its mathematical model can be described as:

4 Experimental Simulation

Based on analyzing the theory and mathematical model of autonomic entrapment system, in order to validate the validity of the ability of object system provides service, this paper simulate function transplant and time sequence function of trap subnet, and analysis the system have or not autonomic trapping mechanism can or not influent the availability of service, average response time and resources utility of object system.

Building the object system and trap subnet which can monitor, analyzing its function, service and connect and trap suspicious information of it. The experiment aims at the conditions of our lab, make concurrent connection request and attack to WEB, DNS and FTP server, observe the difference of service ability of object system when autonomic trapping function is opened or shielded .

When autonomic trapping function is shielded, we cut off the connection of Decoy computer and network and use VU-G1、VU-G2 and VU-G3 access and attack the three network server parallelly, and record the data of the function of server.

For FTP、DNS and WEB servers, when autonomic trap is shielded or opened, we compare the influence of system capability from service availability, average response time and average transmission rate.

(1) Service Availability(SA)

Analyzing each index get from EtherPeek NX, we can get figure 2 shows the change of service availability.

It is obvious that computing resource of server consume greatly, and lead SA of network service descends, when autonomic trapping is shielded, along with the time goes on and the increase of attack, SA of DNS service descends slower, and keep the 70% of availability finally, moreover SA variation curve of FTP and WEB service descends fast, keeping about the 25% of availability finally, it can't provide normal service to user. When autonomic trapping function is opened and system is attacked,

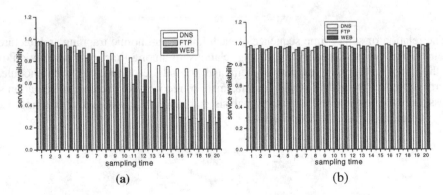

Fig. 2. Availability Variation Curve. (a)Change of Service Availability When Autonomic Trapping is Shielded. (b) Change of Service Availability When Autonomic Trapping is Opened.

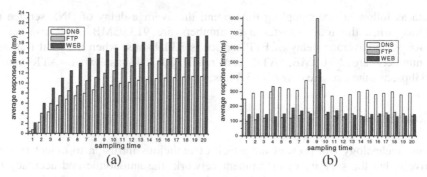

Fig. 3. Variation Curve of Service Average Response Time. (a) Changing of Service Average Response Time When Autonomic Trapping is Shielded. (b) Changing of Service Average Response Time When Autonomic Trapping is Opened.

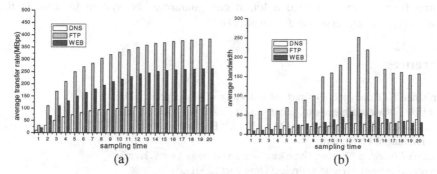

Fig. 4. ATR Variation Curve. (a)ATR When Autonomic Trapping is Shielded. (b) ATR When Autonomic Trapping is Opened. Conclusion.

SA of each server keeps about 95%, and there is not big departure, it shows that autonomic trapping mechanism can prevent malicious attack to occupy the resource of object system, make the network server provide normal service to user.

(2)Service Average Response Time(SART)

The variation curve of SART recorded by EtherPeek NX shows as figure3:

Figure.3(a) shows the changing of SART when autonomic trapping is shielded, when system is attacked, SART of each server increases continually, the comprehensive capability descends integerly, it can't provide normal service to user. Figure 3(b) shows the changing of SART when autonomic trapping is opened, we can see the 95% of network service requests are achieved in 500ms, there are only little proportional request's time is longer, but it can not affect service request. SART of DNS is about 300ms, meet SLA criterion of DNS service; the response time of FTP service and HTTP service keeps about 150ms, meet the request of user.

（3） Average Transfer Rate(ATR)

Figure.4 shows network ATR. Figure.4 （a） shows ATR of DNS, FTP and WEB service when autonomic trapping is shielded they can't satisfy the request of user gradually. Figure.4 （b） shows ATR when autonomic trapping is opened, we can see the data as follow at one sampling time point: the average delay of DNS service is 69.843ms, when the total transfer byte numbers are 913.95MB, ATR can reach 393.840bps; the average delay of FTP service is 330.954ms, when the total transfer byte numbers are 891.9MB, ATR can reach 2017048bps; when ATR reach 246063bps, and the average delay is 65.64ms.

5 Conclusion

Trapping technology can prevent the attack of malicious intrusion to object system effectively, but the security of entrapment network, the autonomic and accuracy of trap course are not been reported. This paper proposes an trapping system with autonomic intrusion tolerance, and makes the theoretical analysis, data modeling and experimental simulation research on it. The result shows the capability of comprehensive service of FTP, DNS and WEB of object system with autonomic trapping function are enhanced a lot, it can guarantee the system to provide the normal service when servers are been attacked.

References

1. Spitzner, L.: Honeypots-Definitions and Value of Honeypots (2001),
   http://www.enteract.com/~lspitz/honeypot.html
2. The Cuckoos Egg. Clifford Stoll Mass Market Publishing (1995)
3. An Evening With Berferd,
   http://www.all.net/books/berferd/berferd.html
4. Project Honeynet Members. Project Honeynet (2001),
   http://project.honeynet.org
5. Horn, P.: Autonomic computing: IBM perspective on the state of information technology. IBM, Armonk, NY (2001)
6. Anthony, R., Pelc, M., Ward, P., et al.: A Run-Time Configurable Software Architecture for Self-Managing Systems. In: The 5th IEEE International Conference on Autonomic Computing, Chicago, IL, USA, June 2-6 (2008)
7. Taleb-Bendiab, A.: Autonomic Computing Meets Complex Information Systems: Theory and Practice. In: WEBIST, Barcelona, Spain, March 3-6 (2007)
8. Kunii, T.L.: Autonomic and Trusted Computing for Ubiquitous Intelligence. In: The 4th International Conference on Autonomic and Trusted Computing (ATC 2007), Hong Kong, China, July 11-13 (2007)
9. Strassner, J., Samudrala, S., Cox, G., et al.: The Design of a New Context-Aware Policy Model for Autonomic Networking. In: The 5th IEEE International Conference on Autonomic Computing, Chicago, IL, USA, June 2-6 (2008)

Improving the Quality of Protection of Web Application Firewalls by a Simplified Taxonomy of Web Attacks

Yi Han[1], Akihiro Sakai[1], Yoshiaki Hori[2], and Kouichi Sakurai[2]

[1] Graduate School of Information Science and Electrical Engineering,
Kyushu University
[2] Faculty of Information Science and Electrical Engineering,
Kyushu University

Abstract. Nowadays, with over 70% of attacks carried out over the web application level, organizations need all the help they can get in making their system secure. Web Application Firewalls (WAFs) are among the tools that are commonly used for the prevention of Web attacks. However, the WAFs provide very little protection on their own. In order to become useful, they must be configured with rules. Unfortunately, the rule configuration process is not easy and error-prone, thus the quality of protection(QoP) of WAFs is still behind our expectations. In this paper, we investigate the current WAFs and point out some of their problems regarding about the poor QoP. We then analyze the origins of these problems and propose two decision modules, the attack-decision module and priority-decision module based on a proposed simplified taxonomy of web attacks which are helpful for improving the QoP of WAFs. Finally, we conclude our work and show future interests to extend our modules to IDS systems.

1 Introduction

Nowadays, with over 70% of attacks carried out over the web application level, organizations need all the help they can get in making their system secure. WAFs are developed to establish an increased external security layer to detect and/or prevent attacks before they reach web application[1]. Generally, it can be an appliance, server plugin, or filter that applies a set of rules to an HTTP conversation. In other words, WAFs provide very little protection on their own without rules. Hence, the configuration of the rules is very important which affect the QoP of WAFs. Unfortunately, the rule configuration process is not easy and error-prone, correspondingly, the QoP of the current WAFs is also not as good as we expect. As a result, we start our research with the motivation of improving the QoP of the WAFs.

Recently, some researches also pointed out the low QoP problems of WAFs[2][4], however, they only pointed out the poor performance or loose design of the WAFs while didn't explain the origins of the problems. After we investigating WAFs, we think that the key point is the policy rules of them. And in

J.H. Park et al. (Eds.): ISA 2009, CCIS 36, pp. 105–110, 2009.
© Springer-Verlag Berlin Heidelberg 2009

our opinion, in order to design useful and effective policy rules, one should understand both web attacks and web applications well enough. But, because the web applications differ a lot, it is nearly impossible and not wise to design one perfect policy rule set for various web applications. But it is reasonable to try best effort to design good policy rule set for one web application, for instance, for only Apache server or for only IIS server. As a result, we'd better make a full understand of the web attacks in order to design better policy rules.

A best and wisest way to understand the web attacks is to examine the taxonomy of the web attacks. As far as we know, there are not too many papers in this field. The main taxonomies of the web attacks is presented in [5] and [6]. In these papers, they proposed the taxonomy of the web attacks from different aspects. Also, they pointed out that the applications, such as WAFs or intrusion detection systems might benefit from the proposed taxonomies. Unfortunately, they didn't explain how to make use of the result further more. In this paper, we modified the existing taxonomies of web attacks and show how to make use of them aiming at improving the QoP of WAFs.

The challenging issues of our research are Find the origins of the poor QoP of WAFs, How to modify the existing taxonomy of web attacks so that the WAFs might benefit from, and item The proposal for improving the QoP of WAFs.

With the purpose of addressing the challenging issues, out main contribution in this paper are propose a simplified taxonomy of web attacks, and propose two decision modules based on the simplified taxonomy of web attacks so that the QoP of WAFs could be improved.

2   Investigation of the Current WAFs

Currently, there are many kinds of WAF products in market. Basically, there are two big categories, open source tools, such as Breach-ModSecurity[1], AQTronix-WebKnight[11], and commercial tools, such as Breach-WebDefend[12], Microsoft-ISA[13]. Among these web application firewalls, ModSecurity of Breach Security Inc is one of the most famous open source WAFs which provides protection from a range of attacks against web applications and allows for HTTP traffic monitoring, logging and real-time analysis. It is also an open source project that aims to make the WAF technology available to everyone. And in this paper, we will take it as an example to explain the detail of WAFs.

WAFs provide three protection strategies. The first is external patching, also known as "just-in-time patching" or "virtual patching". The second is the positive security model which is an independent input validation envelope. And rules must be adjusted to the application. For this strategy, automated and continuous learning in order to adjust for changes is the key. The last strategy is negative security model which is used to look for bad stuff. This model is mostly signatures based. It is generic but requires some tweaking for each application. Although three strategies have been provided, they are still facing the false negative, false positive, low efficiency, etc...

2.1 Poor Quality of Protection

Although the rule is very flexible, it is hard for people to handle them. First of all, the designers can not design a perfect rule set which is suitable for both web applications and web attacks in one time since there will be always false positives or false negatives. Then we should keep on modifying our rules. However, it is not easy to modify or update the rules once they have been configured. If we just add the new rules behind the existed ones, it will bring another problem that the size of the rules becomes larger and larger. In other words, it will take a lot of time checking the messages through the WAFs. How long could we keep on waiting? All these problems can be concluded as poor QoP. For ModSecurity, they also pay attention to such problem and are doing a lot of effort to improve the quality. However, we didn't see any results presented in public.

In our opinion the origins of these problems is that firstly there is not a good instruction system for designing the policy rules. Without a good instruction system, the rule design seems to be in confusion and hard to modify. Secondly, there is no good optimization module for the existing rules. Therefore, a lot of time has been wasted due to the effectiveness checking.

Know yourself and know your enemy, victory is assured. This means that if we want a high QoP, we should understand both web attacks and web applications quite well. We deploy our research from these two directions. We try to make use of the taxonomy of the web attacks or applications to develop some modules for policy rule design and optimization. However, it is not reasonable and impossible to develop some modules which is suitable for all kinds of web applications. But for a web application, it is reasonable and possible to develop some modules in order to design better policy rules. For instance, ModSecurity is mainly used for protecting Apache Server, for such a decided web application we can think about some modules in order to design better rules and optimize them. In this paper, we will make use of the result of the taxonomy of the web attacks to propose two modules aiming at achieving this purpose.

3 Simplified Taxonomy of Web Attacks

A best way to know something fully is to see the taxonomy of it. A taxonomy is a classification scheme that partitions a body of knowledge and defines the relationship of the objects. Classification is the process of using a taxonomy for seperating and ordering. Satisfactory taxonomies have classification categories with the following characteristics:

1. mutually exclusive: classifying in one category excludes all others because categories do not overlap,
2. exhaustive: taken together, the categories include all possibilities,
3. unambiguous: clear and precise so that classification is not uncertain, regardless of who is classifying,

4. repeatable: repeated applications result in the same classification, regardless of who is classifying,
5. accepted: logical and intuitive so that categories could become generally approved,
6. useful: could be used to gain insight into the field of inquiry.

Satisfying these characteristics, there are thousands of papers regarding the taxonomy of computer vulnerability, computer attack, network attack and so on. However, there are not many papars about the taxonomy of the web attacks. As far as we know, there are mainly two kinds of taxonomy of web attacks as showed in [5] and [6]. We define them as taxonomy type A and taxonomy type B respectively. Taxonomy type A is based on the concept of attack life cycle. there are 10 categories for the taxonomy. The attack gets through an entry point, searching for a vulnerability in the web server or web application, which might be exploited to defeat some security service. The vulnerability is realized by an action, using some HTTP verb and headers of certain length, directed against a given target and with a given scope. Different from type A, type B is classified from client-side to server-side. Although they look different, the categories they used are nearly the same, for example, the vulnerability(type of attack in B), HTTP verb(HTTP method in B), Action(Operation in B) and so on. These taxonomies are really helpful for web application firewall policy rule design or optimization since every attack, either know or unknown, could be mapped to them. The challenge issue is that how to use them effectively. We don't think it is wise to design the policies according to each category of taxonomy A or B since it would take the system too much time and not effective. As a result, we propose a simplified taxonomy of web attacks easily for helping to design and optimize the WAF policy rules flexibly and effectively.

Next, we explain how to construct a simplified taxonomy of web attacks based on the existing taxonomy of web attacks. First of all, we extract the most used categories from the existing taxonomy or extract the categories according to the issues people care about, for example the vulnerability, HTTP verb or actions. After that, we take two categories or three categories to construct a plane or a space. We define such plane or space as a simplified taxonomy. The benefit of the simplified taxonomy lies in firstly it is very flexible and easy to perform. Secondly, it can make things very clear and be executed effectively. In this paper we take the Action and HTTP Verb as an example to explain that how to construct such plane.

As Figure 2 shows, we choose the Action and HTTP Verb category to form a new simplified taxonomy plane. For the Action axis, we arrange the items in it according to different severity. For example, we can image the A, B, C, D along this axis as read, search, modify, delete or other actions. The closer the item near to the origin of coordinates, the smaller severity it would be given. We deal with the HTTP Verb axis as the same. Thus we can form a simplified taxonomy plane. And each web attack could be mapped to it. For instance, we mapped web attack X and Y to this plane. We can see that such simplified taxonomy system is very easy and flexible.

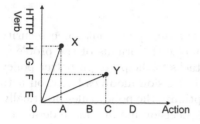

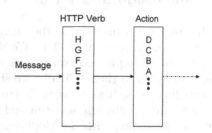

Fig. 1. Simplified Taxonomy of Web Attacks

Fig. 2. Attack-decision Module Method 1

4   Two Decision Modules for WAF

In this section, we will use the proposed simplified taxonomy of web attacks.

4.1   Attack-Decision Module

The attack-decision module is used to check the attack which indicate how to design effective policy rules. Concretely, there are two methods for checking the attacks. One of the methods is described as Figure 3, the attack-decision module will check the coming message step by step according to the chosen categories in simplified taxonomy. Additionally, in each step, the module will check by the severity of the items in this category. In other words, this method is to detect the attack according to the axis one by one in the simplified taxonomy plane. Another method is to detect the attack based on the combination of the chosen categories of the simplified taxonomy of web attack. And this method is to detect the attack according to the whole plane of the simplified taxonomy plane. Designing the policy rules according to such modulo, firstly detection becomes clear and flexible. Secondly, the detection is complete and unambiguous, even the unknown web attacks can be detected. Lastly, the configured policy rule is very easy to update and modify.

4.2   Priority-Decision Module

The priority-decision module is used to decide the priority of the attack. Correspondingly, we could optimize the policy rules according to the priority of the attack. We define the distance from the origin of the coordinate to the attack point in Figure 2 as the priority distance. For instance, the distance of 0X in Figure 2 is the priority of the attack X. The longer the distance is, the higher priority the attack has. Thus we could decide the priority for the known web attacks before we detect them. And the WAF will reset the policy rule list according to the priority of the attacks so that the check time could be reduced. In addition, once the attacks containing both known and unknown attacks have been blocked, we could also use the priority-decision module to classify the attack for a prompt and effective response.

5   Conclusion and Future Work

In this paper, we investigate the current WAFs and point out some security problems which cause poor QoP. We then analyze the origins of the problems and propose a simplified taxonomy of web attacks for help design better policy rules and optimize them. Finally, we show two decision modules based on it to indicate how to use it and how to design and optimize the policy rules practically. In the future, we are interested in making our decision module more detail, for instance, combining with the ModSecurity or other products. Also, we are going to extend our proposal for IDS systems.

References

1. ModSecurity Reference Manual Version 2.5.0, Breach Security, Inc., http://www.breach.com (February 19, 2008)
2. Desmet, L., Piessens, F., Joosen, W., Verbaeten, P.: Bridging the Gap Between Web Application Firewalls and Web Application. In: FMSE 2006, Alexanadria, Virginia, USA, Novermber 3 (2006)
3. Byrne, P.: Application firewalls in a defence-in-depth design. Network Security 2006(9), 9–11 (2006)
4. Forster, K.: Why Firewalls Fail to Protect Web Sites. Lockstep Systems, Inc. (2002)
5. Alvarez, G., Petrovic, S.: A Taxonomy of Web Attacks. In: Cueva Lovelle, J.M., Rodríguez, B.M.G., Gayo, J.E.L., Ruiz, M.d.P.P., Aguilar, L.J. (eds.) ICWE 2003. LNCS, vol. 2722, pp. 295–298. Springer, Heidelberg (2003)
6. Lai, J.-Y., Wu, J.-S., Chen, S.-J., Wu, C.-H., Yang, C.-H.: Designing a Taxonomy of Web Attacks. In: 2008 International Conference on Convergence and Hybrid Information Technology, pp. 278–282 (2008)
7. Almgren, M., Barse, E.L., Jonsson, E.: Consolidation and Evaluation of IDS Taxonomies. In: Nordic Workshop on Secure IT Systems, Norway, October 15-17, 2003, pp. 57–70 (2003)
8. Howard, J.D., Longstaff, T.A.: A Common Language for Computer Security Incidents. Technical Report SAND98-8667, Sandia National Laboratories (1998)
9. Open Web Application Security Project (OWASP), Top ten most critical web application vulnerabilities (2005), http://www.owasp.org/documentation/topten.html
10. Web Application Security Consortium, Web Application Firewall Evaluation Criteria, version 1.0 (January 2006), http://www.webappsec.org/projects/wafec/
11. AQTronix-WebKnight, http://www.aqtronix.com/
12. Breach-WebDefend, http://www.breach.com/products/webdefend.html
13. Microsoft-ISA, http://www.microsoft.com/forefront/edgesecurity/isaserver/en/us/default.aspx

Reconsidering Data Logging in Light of Digital Forensics

Bin-Hui Chou[1,2], Kenichi Takahashi[2], Yoshiaki Hori[2,3], and Kouichi Sakurai[2,3]

[1] Graduate School of Information Science and Electrical Engineering,
Kyushu University, Japan
[2] Institute of Systems, Information Technologies and Nanotechnologies (ISIT), Japan
[3] Faculty of Information Science and Electrical Engineering,
Kyushu University, Japan
chou@itslab.csce.kyushu-u.ac.jp, takahashi@isit.or.jp

Abstract. Logs record the events that have happened within in a system so they are considered the history of system activities. They are one of the objects that digital forensic investigators would like to examine when a security incident happens. However, logs were initially created for trouble shooting, and are not purposefully designed for digital forensics. Thus, enormous and redundant log data make analysis tasks complicated and time-consuming to find valuable information, and make logging-related techniques difficult utilized in some systems such as embedded systems. In this paper, we reconsider a data logging mechanism in terms of forensics and consequently, we propose purpose-based forensic logging. In purpose-based forensic logging, we only collect the required logs according to a specific purpose, which could decrease the space that logs occupy and may mitigate the analysis tasks during forensic investigations.

Keywords: log, evidence acquisition, purpose-based, digital forensics.

1 Introduction

The total damage caused by cyber crimes amounts to 17.5 billion dollars in 2004 [10]. As security incidents are growing, digital forensics as a subject of incident investigation has been becoming more and more important. Digital forensics manages the collection, preservation, analysis, and presentation of digital evidence [3], which encompasses logs, registry, cookies, files, and so on.

Logs are comprised of log entries. Each log entry records a certain event that happened in a system, and consequently, logs are considered the history of system activities. Hence, attackers would try to tamper or delete logs because they do not want to leave any trails indicating their malicious behaviors so [13][14][15] work on protecting the integrity of logs. Furthermore, there are also some papers such as [4][5][6] doing log compression to decrease the space that logs occupy.

Investigators would also aim at logs during the investigation. However, logs are designed for trouble shooting so that logs record system errors, transaction

J.H. Park et al. (Eds.): ISA 2009, CCIS 36, pp. 111–118, 2009.
© Springer-Verlag Berlin Heidelberg 2009

history, etc. and are not purposefully designed for incident investigation. Accordingly, logs contain abundant and redundant data for forensic purposes because they record the chronological sequences of system events. Thus, enormous and redundant logs make analysis tasks complicated and time-consuming to find valuable information. Also, a great deal of logs make logging-related techniques difficult utilized in the systems which have limited memory, CPU resources, and network bandwidth or storage capabilities. Based on these problems, we propose a new logging concept in terms of forensics, named purpose-based forensic logging.

2   Problems of Current Logging

The term log "stems from the practice of floating a stationary log (a wooden block attached to a reel via rope) to provide a fixed point of reference for the purpose of measuring a ship's speed [11]." In computer systems, logs were designed to fix fatal systems errors and to work as journals. Since logs record the activities which happened within a system, they also play an important role in security nowadays. Logs provide an opportunity of discovering anomaly messages which possibly imply attacks. Thus, for a system administrator who gives internal incident reports or a forensic investigator, one of the significant evidence sources he has to watch is logs.

However, logs are not purposefully created for digital forensics although they are one of the good and simple ways to crack an attack case. Accordingly, logs usually contain much information because they record the chronological sequence of system events, while they result in some processing challenges at the same time. One of the challenges is that logs record a wide range of events (i.e. logged-in users, executed programs, etc.) as system journals and thus usually require a large amount of space to store the associated log entries. At times, it can generate thousands of log records every minute. Besides that, various kinds of log information also makes the analyzing task complicated and time-consuming because it is difficult to find the correlation from thousands of log records.

Another of the challenges is that log records contain much redundant information. For example, an operating system's logging system writes system booting, update, and halt information in logs everyday. There may be successive hundreds of lines recording a SSH-login password brute force attack launched by the same malicious attacker in the SSH server log. Furthermore, let us consider an example of what auditing is doing against database intrusion. Typically the database server is set in the center of an organization network to protect the data within it. A connection to the database must pass through the firewall first, then the web server, and so on. All related devices (e.g. firewall) and servers (e.g. web and database server) log this access, and they all can provide the identity of this access. These redundant records can be the investigation source for investigators or administrators while they also occupy much space but provide the similar information. Let us look at a real world attack case as follows.

"On the morning of March 1st, 2007, an authorized user connecting from IP 192.168.1.20 executed a successful brute force attack against PRODSQL05 server. Once access was gained to the database, a connection was made using Microsoft OSQL client to create a backdoor account [7]."

There are two attacks in the above case: one is a successful brute force attack; the other is the creation of a backdoor account. Current logs contain the system event records while only a small part of them divulge the message of attacks. Hence, even if we only have the record of error login messages instead of recording everything, we can still know the brute force attack because brute force attacks apparently result in duplicated login trials. Except login error logs, the rest of logs are fruitless for associating with the brute force attack. If we have the logs that record the addition of an account, then we can get a piece of evidence that an attacker has created a backdoor account.

Thus, we consider a new logging concept in terms of forensics, named purpose-based forensic logging. All system activities are recorded in the current logging while in purpose-based forensic logging, different purposes are defined and only required logs are recorded based on each specific purpose.

3 Purpose-Based Forensic Logging

3.1 Collectable Logs

In this paper, we try to find out what kinds of logs or logged value are required according to a specific purpose (e.g. intrusion detection, unauthorized access). Thus, it will reduce the amount of logs and help analysis tasks to know correlation between logs and each specific purpose.

In this paper, we use database logs as our examination target as the first step to design purpose-based forensic logging. To protect the data in a database, database should never be directly exposed to the public Internet [9], but in the core of the organization architecture as Fig. 1. It is an example of the path, where a database access is sent after requested by a user. Along the request of a database access, that is, from the firewall, the web server, to the database, a variety of logs are recorded.

For instance, the following is an example of firewall logs.

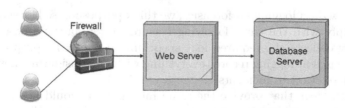

Fig. 1. An access to the database

March 02, 2007 07:39:08 Unrecognized attempt blocked from 192.168.1.20
TCP:43646

Firewall logs contain the information of the timestamps, packets blocked or passed, the source IP address, requested protocol and port.

In web server logs, they include the information relating to the HTTP request, inclusive of source IP address, timestamps, page requested, HTTP code, bytes served, user agent, and referer. In some systems, the data are separated into distinct logs, such as access log, error logs, or referer log. An typical example of web server logs is as follows.

192.168.1.20 - - [20/Jan/2009:16:56:02 -0400] "GET /contacts.html
HTTP/1.0" 200 4595 "-" "http://www.kyushu-u.ac.jp/" "Mozillar/4.05
(Macintosh; I; PPC)"

Database logs include transaction logs, system event logs, SQL error logs, redo logs, and so on. For instance, SQL error logs are basically like the following example. Similar log entries appear repeatedly.

2007-03-02 07:39:08.80 Logon Login failed for user 'sa'. [Client: 192.168.1.20]
2007-03-02 07:39:09.00 Logon Error: 18456, severity: 14, state: 8.
2007-03-02 07:39:09.20 Logon Login failed for user 'sa'. [Client: 192.168.1.20]
2007-03-02 07:39:09.40 Logon Error: 18456, severity: 14, state: 8.

We can see that most logs are recorded in order to fix a certain system fatal error when performing some updates and to record process transactions, however most of them may not be necessary for digital forensics. For example, what investigators would like to know is the data implying who, and attackers' actions. Hence, '192.168.10.15,' 'GET /contact.html,' 'Login failed,' etc. in the above three examples are spotlighted during the investigation, and the rest parts in the above logs are scarcely concerned. Moreover, the 'login failed' message shows twice in the above example and much more records in the complete logs, and actually we just need one record to represent someone keeps trying the account. Because the administrator can establish the policy of the firewall such as "Block repeated failed logins from the same IP address" so we can find the firewall log and database log show the same event.

3.2 Features

To design new data logging for forensics, we think purpose-based forensic logging should comply with the three following features. First, purpose-based forensic logging only collects the required logs according to a specific purpose. This is because the current logging records everything without considering most of those logs are not relevant to incidents.

Second, the logs that provide the same information should not be collected repeatedly, which means the redundant logs are cast aside. We showed that there are many records along the connection from the firewall to the database in

Fig. 1 which stand for the intruder's identity. The IP address in the firewall log, web server's system event log and the database's transaction log, etc., we can find trails indicating intruder's identity from these logs. For instance, if we just collect the IP address from the database's transaction log, then we will be able to identify the intruder's source. Accordingly, other logs (i.e. logs in the firewall or web server) appears to be redundant for this purpose (i.e. knowing where the attacker comes from or who he is).

Last, logs recorded in purpose-based forensic logging is not confined to the current log data because we think it is not sufficient to investigate an incident with current logs occasionally. For example, POST data in HTTP protocol is even not an option in Windows IIS (Internet Information Services) servers although POST data provide insight into web application attacks [12]. Therefore, additional logs (POST data) which are not recorded in the current logging system are essential, and then purpose-based forensic logging should indicate the requisite information which encompasses not only the current logs but also the data which are not included in the current logging such as POST data, system call records, executed process history, and so forth. Then, we can build some countermeasures to record those information (e.g. POST data).

3.3   Purpose and Log

In purpose-based forensic logging, it is essential to find the relationship between logs and purposes so we have to map logs to each specific purpose. In order to correlate logs and purposes, we define purposes as the first step. However, purposes are often abstract so it is difficult to map logs directly to purposes. Thus, we use forward reasoning to analyze each purpose and consequently, we try to break purposes down into some subgroups. The subgroups of purposes could be the components of purposes, or the causes of them.

For instance, the purpose, *unauthorized access* is comprised of *approach* and *damage*. This is because attackers must exploit at least one approach to access a system without authorization, and the attack must result in some damage to the system. We also describe them with a relation of cause and effect. That is, if we could know either the *approach* adopted by attackers or the *damage* caused by attackers, then we can say *unauthorized access* has happened in the system. The *approach* that attackers exploit to access a machine can be divided into *attack on password, SQL injection,* etc.; *attack on password* can be divided into *guessing* and *stealing* of password further. For example, attackers must use some methods to exploit a potential system vulnerability on *guessing* of password so it is comprised of *brute force* and *dictionary* attacks. By analyzing a specific purpose using forward reasoning, we can transform it in a more and more concrete way and narrow it down so finally we can have the required log data. Based on this idea, we analyze the components of purposes or the reasons resulting in attacks.

The example of unauthorized access case is shown in Fig. 2. We notate the required log data we need for a specific purpose by pointing with an arrow and forward reasoning parts by connecting with lines. Unauthorized access is

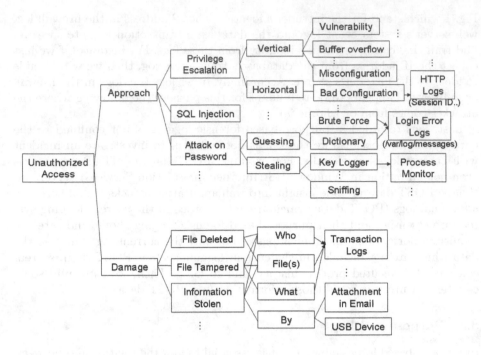

Fig. 2. An example of purpose-based forensic logging

considered to be caused by some attacks such as *attacks on password, privilege escalation* and so forth. We can break *privilege escalation* down into *vertical* and *horizontal* privilege escalation further (Fig. 2).

For example, we break attacks on password down and get the *guessing* and *stealing* of password, and in the *guessing* of password, *brute force* attacks and *dictionary* attack (Fig. 2) should be considered. In the brute force attack on password, attackers try logging in to the database until they successfully log in, so error records of login failure (e.g. written in /var/log/messages in Unix-like systems) must be generated repeatedly when attackers perform the brute force attack. Therefore, we can know the attack has happened from login error logs.

We categorize the *damage* caused by unauthorized access into *file deleted, file tampered, information stolen*, and so on (Fig. 2). In the case of *file deleted*, what we concern is who deleted which file(s), so we put lines between *file deleted* and *who*, and *file deleted* and *file(s)*. We can discover the evidence from transaction logs so what we should collect here is transaction logs. Moreover, in the example of information stolen, we should consider who leaked the private information or file by attaching it in a sending mail or smuggling it by USB devices.

For instance, in the case of *stealing* password by using *keyloggers*, the current logs cannot provide the evidence which proves a keylogger exists in a system because a keylogger usually runs as resident program in the main memory when the operating system starts up. Therefore, we have to preserve other data as evidence. Fortunately, since process monitor can provide the information about what processes are being executed, we can edit a subroutine which acquires the result of process monitor in purpose-based forensic logging. Also, the registry used in Windows systems records which processes are installed in the machine so it is possible to find the evidence of keylogger from the registry as well.

4   Conclusion and Future Work

Because current logging implementations and methods are not designed originally for forensics, we proposed a new data logging concept, named purpose-based forensic logging in this paper. In purpose-based forensic logging, only required log and values are collected and the redundant or irrelevant logs are excluded according to each specific purpose, we can reduce the amount of logs. Reduced amount of logs could also lessen the difficulty of analyzing logs.

In this paper, we have shown our preliminary result towards purpose-based forensic logging, but we should expand the discussion of it by analyzing purposes, attacks and required information from different kinds of views. Moreover, we will evaluate the effect of log reduction after employing purpose-based forensic logging.

Acknowledgments. This research was partially supported by NICT International Collaborative Research Grant.

References

1. Kent, K., Souppaya, M.: Guide to Computer Security Log Management. National Institute of Standards and Technology (NIST), USA (2006)
2. Carrier, B., Spafford, E.: Getting Physical with the Digital Investigation Process. International Journal of Digital Evidence (2003)
3. Carreir, B.: File System Forensic Analysis. Addison-Wesley, Reading (2005)
4. Balakrishnan, R. , Sahoo, R. K.: Lossless Compression for Large Scale Cluster Logs. IBM Research Report RC23902 (W0603-038) (2006)
5. Rácz, B., Lukács, A.: High density compression of log files. In: IEEE Data Compression Conference. Snowbird, UT, USA (2004)
6. Skibiński, P., Swacha, J.: Fast and efficient log file compression. In: Ioannidis, Y., Novikov, B., Rachev, B. (eds.) ADBIS 2007. LNCS, vol. 4690, pp. 56–69. Springer, Heidelberg (2007)
7. Fowler, K.: A Real World Scenario of a SQL Server 2005 Database Forensics Investigation. In: 2007 Black Hat USA (2007)
8. Fowler, K.: SQL Server Database Forensics. In: 2007 Black Hat USA (2007)
9. Natun, R.B.: Implementing Database Security and Auditing. Elsevier, Amsterdam (2005)
10. Computer Crime Research Center, CSI/FBI Computer Crime and Security Survey (2004), http://www.crime-research.org/news/11.06.2004/423
11. Etymology of Log, Wikipedia, http://en.wikipedia.org/wiki/Data_log

12. Belani, R., Willis, C.: Web Application Incident Response and Forensics: A Whole New Ball Game. In: OWASP AppSec Conference (2006)
13. Kawaguchi, N., Ueda, S., Obata, N., Miyaji, R., Kaneko, S., Shigeno, H., Okada, K.: A Secure Logging Scheme for Forensic Computing. In: Proceedings of the 2004 IEEE Workshop on Information Assurance (2004)
14. Schneier, B., Kelsey, J.: Secure Audit Logs to Support Computer Forensics. ACM Transactions on Information and System Security 2, 159–176 (1999)
15. Bellare, M., Yee, B.S.: Forward Integrity for Secure Audit Logs. University of California, San Diego (1997)

Blurriness in Live Forensics: An Introduction

Antonio Savoldi and Paolo Gubian

Department of Electronics for Automation, University of Brescia
Via Branze 38, I25121 Brescia, Italy
{antonio.savoldi,paolo.gubian}@ing.unibs.it

Abstract. The Live Forensics discipline aims at answering basic questions related to a digital crime, which usually involves a computer-based system. The investigation should be carried out with the very goal to establish which processes were running, when they were started and by whom, what specific activities those processes were doing and the state of active network connections. Besides, a set of tools needs to be launched on the running system by altering, as a consequence of the Locard's exchange principle [2], the system's memory. All the methodologies for the live forensics field proposed until now have a basic, albeit important, weakness, which is the inability to quantify the perturbation, or blurriness, of the system's memory of the investigated computer. This is the very last goal of this paper: to provide a set of guidelines which can be effectively used for measuring the uncertainty of the collected volatile memory on a live system being investigated.

1 Introduction

The Digital forensics science strives to define methodologies and best practices which can be used to face the increasing demand for investigations posed by cybercrime. Apart from the well-known post-mortem paradigms of analysis, used for many years, the live forensics approach is emerging as the new standard when dealing with critical computer systems, such as those which regard mission-critical fields [3]. Thus, the very goal of this applied discipline is to collect evidential data from the computer's memory in order to define the state at the time when an incident occurred. Naturally, the act of collecting data from a live system causes changes that a forensic investigator will need to document and explain with regard to the impact on the digital evidence. For instance, running a tool like the well-known *dd* [4] from a removable media device will certainly alter volatile data when it is loaded into main memory. Another example could concern the Helix tool [5], which can create or modify files and Registry entries on the system being investigated. Similarly, using remote forensic tools necessarily establishes a network connection, executes instructions in the memory, and makes other alterations on the evidentiary system.

Until now, by looking at the standard scientific literature that regards digital forensics, there is no mention of what could be the extent of the memory's impact caused by running tools, when a live investigation needs to be performed. Moreover, all the proposed methodologies regarding live forensics consider modifications of the system's memory as a marginal problem. Indeed, such approaches are not able to quantify, or at

J.H. Park et al. (Eds.): ISA 2009, CCIS 36, pp. 119–126, 2009.

least to define a range of the perturbation on the system's memory caused by the running tools. Only vague and imprecise opinions have been provided with the result that nobody, especially attorneys and judges, is aware of the real impact of a running tool on the memory of a live system. This is the very goal of this research paper: to provide a reasonable and realistic overview of the uncertainty of a live forensic analysis, by quantifying the extent of such modification on the system's memory. Moreover, examples of blurriness, which defines how much the memory has been affected by a tool, will be presented, giving also a solid base to understand the basic factors that influence this parameter. Finally, some guidelines to approach the problem will be pointed out with regard to state-of-the-art computer systems.

2   Meaning of Blurriness

When dealing with a live forensic case, care must be taken to minimize changes made to the system, by collecting the most volatile data, according to the order of volatility described in detail in RFC 3227 [6]. Usually, the investigator should be aware of what to collect when a digital live investigation has to be performed. Relevant data, both volatile and non-volatile, are defined as follows.

- Volatile Data: they can be defined as critical system details that provide the investigator with insight as to how the system was compromised and the nature of the compromise. Examples include logged in users, active network connections and the processes running on the system. Other data are represented by ephemeral information that is not critical in identifying system status and details. This information will be beneficial to the investigation and will provide further insight to the nature and purpose of the infection. Examples of this data include scheduled tasks and clipboard contents.
- Non-Volatile Data: they reveal the status, settings and configuration of the target system, potentially providing clues as to the method of compromise and infection of the system or network. Examples of this data include registry settings and audit policy. Other data of this category provide historical information and context to support the understanding of the nature and purpose of the infection, but is not critical in the system status, settings or configuration. Examples of this data include system event logs and Web browser history.

However, live data can be collected in different ways, both hardware and software, which differ in terms of fidelity, atomicity and integrity. For instance, let us consider the collection of the system's memory. As pointed out in [7], fidelity implies the ability to collect the real, bit-by-bit content of the RAM memory. In fact, hardware based approaches promise precise fidelity through the use of an external and trusted hardware channel, and exclusive access to the memory of the host. Conversely, software approaches cannot guarantee the same level of fidelity because of the modification caused by the process running in the memory being collected. Moreover, the snapshot of memory should be acquired by means of an atomic operation, which implies the collection of the whole observable memory without interruptions made by other processes. The software based approach of accessing memory, copying it, and then writing it out by an IO channel, while the OS and other applications continue to remain active, results in the memory image being imprecise, and not attributable to a specific point in time. Rather, such a memory image will be "blurred", or partially modified, as a result of the active processes of the operating system. However, hardware methods promise atomic snapshots by guaranteeing that all CPUs will be switched off for the period of memory collection. Last but not least, the integrity of the memory being collected cannot be assured by means of software approaches, such as the *dd* tool. In fact, the reading process could not alter OS's data structures or kernel memory space directly. As a matter of fact, the OS's memory of the system under analysis undergoes numerous changes as a direct result of the imaging processes action. For instance, the page cache is normally used for dealing with almost every I/O operation, such as those related to reading and writing a file.

It is worth mentioning that memory imaging tools, such as *dd*, can be really useful and, in many cases, the only viable solution for acquiring the RAM memory of a system under analysis. On the other hand, we should be aware, or at least have a rational and repeatable procedure, of how much the host memory will be affected as a result of the imaging process. Alterations caused by software imaging approaches can be thought of as a consequence of the well-known Locard's exchange principle [2], which states that a system being observed will be affected by the measuring process itself. In fact, the word "blurriness" can well exemplify this concept: the alteration caused by the measuring process onto an arbitrary live system, not necessarily a computer based one, will produce an error on the measure itself, caused by the convolution of the measurement tool impulse function with the property of the system (e.g. affected pages) that we want to measure. More precisely, if we define as $x(t)$ the property we want to measure and $h(t)$ the measurement impulse function, we can state that the resulting property we measure can be expressed as $y(t) = x(t) \star h(t)$.

This is a general problem in measurement science. An analogy to this would be in astronomy, where we would like to measure the size of an object (e.g. meteor), but the telescope we have (measurement tool) is blurry (e.g. the first version of Hubble telescope). If we look at a distant star, we see a blur of a certain diameter, which is a good approximation of the impulse function, the width of the blur being close to zero. The image we get with a point source is basically the convolution of the measurement system (the telescope) with the impulse function (the spot caused by the distant star). Now, we look at a closer object (e.g. meteor) that is closer and has a measurable width. We will see a slightly bigger blur (not the real one) which is basically the true picture of the meteor convoluted with the same impulse function.

In our case, if we aim at measuring the impact of a tool on a live system's memory, we need to define a measurement tool. When dealing with the measurement of a computer's volatile memory (e.g. RAM contents) via software, it seems reasonable to use a tool for sampling the whole memory, like *dd* does. Clearly, the *dd* process will cause a memory change which we need to take into account. A possible way to do this is to take memory snapshots back-to-back by measuring the binary difference between different snapshots, to take into account the uncertainty caused by the measurement tool. Particularly, by taking a series of memory snapshots and measuring the statistical variation we can define a more robust measure of the uncertainty caused by the measurement tool. Indeed, the state change of the system, that is how many memory pages have been affected by the imaging process, is like an impulse function, according to the general system theory, because it captures the measured property (the state change of the system) under the impulse condition, that is when we assume no deliberate change in the system. In this case the blurriness is purely due to the measurement process itself. Conversely, when we have a deliberate change on the measurement property (e.g. from running other forensic tools) we effectively convolute the real change with our measurement system and measure a slightly wider blur, like the telescope image.

It should be evident that this approach is an approximation and is based on the assumption that we can consider the ordinary blurriness of the measurement tool, *dd* in our case, as if it is the only one on the running system. In fact, this hypothesis implies that the blurriness of the *dd* tool, the impulse function, should be determined only by the *dd* process itself, without considering any other process of the live system under examination. As a matter of fact, as the experimental results will show, the communication channel used to copy memory snapshots to an external storage device, which is managed by the kernel of the operating system, impacts severely on the blurriness of the measurement tool. On the other hand, we should be aware of how much memory is usually affected when using the *dd* imaging tool.

3 Experimental Setup

Having explained the concept of blurriness, we are ready to prove that on a computer-based system we can measure such a parameter with respect to the volatile memory.

In order to properly evaluate the blurriness caused by the *dd* tool we have taken a series of memory snapshots back-to-back in both real and virtual systems, to highlight whether the communication channels behave similarly with respect to a real and virtual case. All the snapshots were copied respectively to an external USB 2.0 storage device and to another computer system by means of a network link (100 Mbps LAN) to evaluate how the communication channel impacts on the memory blurriness. Up to now we have considered only the USB and the LAN link. In future works we should also consider other kinds of channels, such as the firewire and e-SATA one. Table 1 refers to the case where snapshots were taken from a real Windows XP SP2-based system, equipped with 1.23 Gbytes of RAM, and copied to an external USB 2.0 hard disk. As the table illustrates, we can consider the binary difference between two consecutive snapshots as a measure of the blurriness of the *dd* tool. Particularly, $\Delta\%$ quantifies the percentage difference between two consecutive snapshots. As a matter of fact, this "ordinary" blurriness determines the maximum resolution available to observe the impact of other processes onto the system's memory. Moreover, we cannot measure the blurriness caused by another tool with a better resolution than the one of the "probing" tool. Thus, we must be aware of methods to obtain the best possible resolution in quantifying the normal blurriness which is caused by the *dd* tool.

For the initial part of the experiment, which is devoted to measuring the normal blurriness of the *dd* tool by using the USB 2.0 communication channel, every memory dump was collected, on average, in 80 seconds, and we considered a statistically meaningful,

Table 1. Blurriness of *dd* tool. Snapshots were copied onto an external USB 2.0 drive.

Snapshot #	Different Pages	Equal Pages	$\Delta[\%]$
1 - 2	132430	190961	40.9
3 - 4	131254	192137	40.5
5 - 6	131602	191789	40.7
7 - 8	141924	181467	43.9
9 - 10	133220	190171	41.2

Table 2. Blurriness of *dd* tool. The snapshot were copied to a Linux based system via LAN.

Snapshot #	Different Pages	Equal Pages	$\Delta[\%]$
1 - 2	25688	297703	7.9
3 - 4	24100	299291	7.4
5 - 6	26888	296503	8.3
7 - 8	28440	294951	8.8
9 - 10	23547	299844	7.3

albeit small, set of snapshots to account for statistical variation. So far, the blurriness can be quantified as $B = \mu_{\texttt{diff}} \pm \sigma_{\texttt{diff}}$, where $\mu_{\texttt{diff}}$ is the average of different snapshot pages related to the whole set of snapshots, while $\sigma_{\texttt{diff}}$ refers to the variance of different pages. Thus, we have $B = 134086 \pm 3978$ pages, or $B = 523.8 \pm 15.5$ Mbytes. In other terms, we have about 41.4% of memory modified by the imaging tool.

Similarly, Table 2 refers to the same real Windows-based system where the snapshots were transferred via LAN to a Linux box, by means of the *netcat* tool. Every snapshot was copied, on average, in 120 seconds and the blurriness can be quantified as $B = 25733 \pm 1795$ pages, or $B = 100.5 \pm 7$ Mbytes, which is around 8% of the memory. As the results show, there is a considerable difference in blurriness between this case and the previous one. This is due to the buffer allocation in Windows kernel space, which depends on the communication channel which has been used. We can observe that the former case, as illustrated in Table 1, has a blurriness which is 5 times greater than the latter one. More study would be necessary to determine whether it is possible to control and reduce the buffer at the kernel level, or at least to sort out a better way of transferring a memory snapshot by controlling the memory buffer in kernel space.

As the results show, from the blurriness point of view we should prefer the LAN link to transfer memory snapshots. In fact, we have noticed that the Ethernet driver impacts less than the USB one onto the system's memory. Accepting a blurriness of 5%, on average, over 1 Gbyte of RAM memory implies that the probing tool, in our case *dd*, should be able to "measure" the blurriness of other tools, such as the set of tools in the Helix forensic distribution, with a better resolution than it has. This fact can be easily understood by thinking of the example of the blurred telescope which has been discussed in the previous section. It is not possible to take a measure of an object with a higher resolution than the one that the probing tool has.

After this initial part we have evaluated the blurriness of the *dd* tool on a virtual system, based on Suse Linux 11.1 and equipped with 512 Mbytes of RAM, by transferring memory snapshots initially via USB 2.0 (emulated by VMWare) and after that via

Table 3. Blurriness of the *dd* tool related to a virtual system with 512 Mbytes of RAM (USB transfer)

Snapshot #	Different Pages	Equal Pages	$\Delta[\%]$
1 - 2	30829	100243	23.5
3 - 4	29812	101260	22.7
5 - 6	33111	97961	25.3
7 - 8	35267	95805	26.9
9 - 10	31140	99932	23.8

Table 4. Blurriness of *dd* tool related to a virtual system with 512 Mbytes of RAM (LAN transfer)

Snapshot #	Different Pages	Equal Pages	$\Delta[\%]$
1 - 2	7735	123337	5.9
3 - 4	6599	124473	5.0
5 - 6	6023	125049	4.6
7 - 8	5752	125320	4.4
9 - 10	5547	299844	4.2

Table 5. Blurriness of the *dd* tool related to a virtual system with 512 Mbytes of RAM (USB transfer) with 100% of CPU load

Snapshot #	Different Pages	Equal Pages	$\Delta[\%]$
1 - 2	45089	85983	34.4
3 - 4	46100	84972	35.2
5 - 6	46565	84507	35.5
7 - 8	46089	84983	35.1
9 - 10	46784	84288	35.7

LAN, to highlight differences compared with real systems. In this case the blurriness is $B = 32032 \pm 1939$ pages, or $B = 125.1 \pm 7.6$ Mbytes (24.4%), which is less than the previous case related to a real Windows system. Every snapshot was copied to an external USB sotrage device on average in 25 seconds. Table 3 illustrates experimental results related to the mentioned virtual system.

In this case the blurriness is $B = 6331 \pm 742$ pages, or $B = 24.7 \pm 2.9$ Mbytes (4.8%). Every single memory snapshot was copied onto the host system via *netcat* on average in 40 seconds. As the experimental results shown in Table 4 illustrate, the blurriness is comparable with that on a real system when LAN link is used.

In the last case, which can be seen in Table 5, we wanted to verify how much the CPU load impacts on the blurriness via USB, with respect to the virtual box previously examined. The CPU load was set to 100% with a Perl script with the purpose to occupy the free memory with known data. In this case the blurriness is $B = 46125 \pm 584$ pages, or $B = 180.1 \pm 2.28$ Mbytes (35.2%). Every single memory snapshot was copied onto the host system via *netcat* on average in 35 seconds. As the experimental results shown in Table 5 illustrate, the blurriness is higher than in the previous case. This is not surprising, since the script impacts considerably on the memory coherence, by writing known data to the memory.

Having analyzed the possible resolution of the software probing tool *dd*, which sets the basis to analyze the blurriness of other tools, we can consider how much a forensic procedure can impact onto the memory of a real live system. For such purpose, we have used the Helix forensic distribution on a Windows-based virtual box, equipped with 512 Mbytes of RAM and 10 Gbytes of hard drive. Initially, a full memory snapshot has been collected by means of the *dd* tool. The snapshot was transferred onto an external Linux box via LAN in order to minimize the blurriness caused by the imaging tool.

After that, we used the Windows Forensic ToolChest (WFT) incident response bundle, which is included in Helix. This software package includes different tools which can also alter the Windows registry, and other configuration files. After 45 minutes, the full analysis was completed.

At the end, a second memory snapshot was collected and copied onto the external box. By comparing the two snapshots we have noticed that the memory was changed almost completely, about 97%. Which are the consequences? Without an initial snapshot of the memory, which is altered by definition in about 5%, we have no chance of detecting hidden rootkits which are becoming the new curse for forensic practitioners. More and more rootkits, both in user and kernel memory space, are being developed to subvert the OS behavior. As a consequence, it is mandatory to be aware of how much blurriness we should expect according to the forensic toolkit we are using.

3.1   How to Approach This Issue?

As far as we have seen, blurriness, which is the uncertainty of the affected memory caused by a live forensic tool, can be experimentally quantified. With regard to the *dd* tool, which might be used like a probe to examine the effect of other tools, it should be clear that the blurriness depends on the communication channel. In fact, the way of managing different communication links, which is done with a different page cache policies, impacts strongly on the resulting memory snapshot. Conversely, a LAN link is managed by the kernel in a different way, giving a lower impact on the memory, as a consequence of the different policy for memory allocation in kernel space.

What we are looking for is a precise analysis of this problem which has quite a heavy impact on digital forensics. One direction of research is to understand how to control and, possibly, quantify the blurriness on different operating systems (e.g. Linux and Windows XP).

4   Conclusions

This paper is motivated by the lack of knowledge with respect to the blurriness in live forensics, a discipline that is becoming more and more important in digital investigations. The concept of blurriness applied to the forensics discipline has been pointed out and defined. If we are constrained to examine a system via software (e.g. a mission critical web server), it is essential to collect the memory contents by means of an imaging tool (e.g. *dd*) with a known blurriness. Experimental results show that the USB link affects heavily the blurriness of every tool which uses such a channel of communication.

In this case, the major cause of the memory modification is related to how the communication channel is managed by the OS and not, as could be thought, to the memory allocated by the tool. More research needs to be conducted on this important topic.

References

1. Carrier, B., Grand, F.: A Hardware-Based Memory Acquisition Procedure for Digital Investigations. Digital Investigation 1(1), 50–60 (2004)
2. Chisum, W., Turvey, B.: Evidence Dynamics: Locard's Exchange Principle and Crime Reconstruction. Journal of Behavioral Profiling 1(1) (2000)
3. Savoldi, A., Gubian, P.: Volatile Memory Collection and Analysis for Windows Mission-Critical Computer Systems. International Journal Digital Crime and Forensics 1(3) (2009)
4. Garner, G.M.: Forensics Acquisition Utilities (2008),
   http://www.gmgsystemsinc.com/fau/
5. Helix 3: Helix 3 - Incident Response, Electronic Discovery, Computer Forensics Live CD (2008), http://www.e-fense.com/helix/
6. rfc3227: Guidelines for Evidence Collection and Archiving (2002),
   http://www.ietf.org/rfc/rfc3227.txt
7. Schatz, B.: BodySnatcher: Towards Reliable Volatile Memory Acquisition by Software. In: 7th annual Digital Forensics Research Workshop, pp. 126–134 (2007)

Author Index